The Holy Spirit
IN ME,
THROUGH ME,
and
AROUND ME

The Holy Spirit
IN ME,
THROUGH ME,
and
AROUND ME

Vicki Robinette

XULON PRESS

Xulon Press
2301 Lucien Way #415
Maitland, FL 32751
407.339.4217
www.xulonpress.com

Scripture quotations taken from the Holy Bible, New International Version (NIV). Copyright © 1973, 1978, 1984, 2011 by Biblica, Inc.™. Used by permission. All rights reserved.

Paperback ISBN-13: 978-1-6628-1161-6
Ebook ISBN-13: 978-1-6628-1162-3

DEDICATION

I dedicate this book to my daughter and son-in-law Melissa and Marc Carroll; my son and daughter-in-law Rodney and Alison Smith; my grandchildren Andrew, Megan, and Brandon. I have only been able to see you a few times each year since the Lord has called me away from my home in Michigan. I have missed a lot of family time together, cooking, baking for all of you, and being able to spend special time with you. Thank you for understanding that I had to listen to the Lord and do what He called me to do. God may never let me move back with family, but I love you all and look forward to spending eternity with you.

TABLE OF CONTENTS

1

I AM

In the beginning, GOD! *(Psalms 139: 16, Your eyes saw me when I was formless; all my days were written in your book and planned before a single one of them began. CSB).* Mother was very rebellious when she was young and often ran away from home. Grandpa would end up finding her and making her go back home. Although grandpa, mother's father, was a Latter-Day Saint minister, I have heard he did not live out the Christ-like life in front of his family. Mother and her two brothers did not have a godly example to follow in their home.

I am here because God is sovereign, and it was His plan for me to live and be alive today. If it had been left up to my mother, I would not be alive. While married to Dad, Mother was unfaithful to Dad. During this time, she had several abortions. When Dad realized she was pregnant with me, he would not let her abort me. So, I was born and ended up being my mother's only living child.

Dad was a welder, so we moved around a lot to where the jobs were. At one point, after I was born, we lived in a trailer park. After Dad would leave for work, mother would leave me by myself all day to go off with other men. There was a lady, however, who lived in the trailer next to ours. She would at times keep a watch out for me. When Mom would leave, the neighbor would come and get me keeping me until Dad got home from work. This went on until I was about four years old. As I grew up, I had flashbacks of memories from this time. I asked Dad about many of these faint memories. He often confirmed that what was coming to my mind really happened.

I remember an incident from when I was about four years old and asked my father about it. At the trailer park where we lived, there was also a rooming house where single men lived. I remember following Mom to that house and her talking with a man. That man yelled at me to get home so my mother could go up to his room with him. I remember being scared and I ran. Mom did not come after me. My dad confirmed my memory that there was a rooming house for men in the trailer park where we lived.

When I was four years old, Dad reached his limit with Mom's shenanigans. He decided he was going to leave my mom, and we were going to go live with his family. Dad called his mom and sister to come and get me. He wanted me taken care of while he settled things with Mom. When my grandma and aunt arrived at the trailer park, I was playing off by myself in a pile of dirt. My mother was nowhere to be found. Dad sent me home with them. When my mother came home, she found that dad had packed up her things. He gave her some money and put her on a bus to wherever she wanted to go.

So, Dad and I lived with Grandpa and Grandma for a couple of years. It was then that I started going to church with Grandma. We went to a little church called Cherry Street Baptist Church in Midland, Michigan. I started hearing about the Lord there. However, I did not see the Christian life lived out at home. Grandpa would get drunk, and Grandma would get mad and throw a glass or whatever object was close at him. I started learning it was best if I went off by myself to play. I came from a totally dysfunctional family on both sides.

I had always had a great love for animals and grew to prefer being with animals rather than people. I have always had a strong love for animals, and that love grew stronger as I grew older. I learned that animals really do love people when they are treated with love and kindness. Dad got me a collie when we were living with Grandma and Grandpa. I spent a lot of time with that dog. He ended up dying with distemper when he was about a year old. I still remember the vet and my dad trying their best to save my dog. I was heartbroken.

I did not see much of my mother or her family when I was little. She and one of her husbands or men friends would sometimes show up at my grandparents to see me. If they were drunk, Dad would send them away. I started seeing my mother and her family on a more regular basis when I was in my mid-teens. My mother and I eventually developed a relationship about the time I got married. I can remember one thing my dad told me from the time I was little. It had to have come from God. Dad told me not to hate my mother, that one day she would need me. She did come back into my life, and I did not hate her. We did a lot together in later years when she was no longer married. Her fourth husband died, and she lived alone the last several years of her life. She became part of my life and my children's lives until she passed away. My mother's brother, Uncle Bob, came from Florida to Michigan for her funeral. After the funeral, Uncle Bob told me a lot about my mother during the years I was not with her.

I did not question my mother much about her life.

One thing I did ask my mother in later years was how I got my name. I was named Victoria I with no period after the I. I figured my name Victoria came from my father who was Victor and thought the "I" was after my mother who was named Ila. But she said, "No, I picked out your middle name after the Great I AM". I was shocked. Who would have imagined she would have thought of such a name in that time of her life? I was forty-eight years old when I started reading my Bible, and it came to me how important names were. I know the Lord had to have put that in her mind. The Great I AM, knew there would be a day when I would know the Lord as my Father, know He loved me, and know He wanted me. When everyone else would fail me, the Lord would always be there with me. I cannot tell how many times knowing this has held me together when the different crises would come in my life.

Dad and I lived with his parents until I turned six years old when he remarried. He and Onalee, Mom to me, were married the rest of Dad's life. He passed away at ninety-two. My mom is still living in a nursing home, and she sometimes knows who we are.

After Dad and Mom (Onalee) were married, we would attend church for a while, then dad would get mad about something trivial, and we would not go back again. With Dad's work we moved a lot. Sometimes there would be a couple of years when we did not go to church. I did not attend a church on a regular basis until I was able to drive myself to church without depending on my parents to take me. When I was able to drive myself to church, I started attending Freeland Baptist Church in Freeland, Michigan. I had a desire to know the Lord, but my walk with the Lord was not as deep of a commitment as it would later become. I had no clue how personal and intimate a relationship the Lord would draw me into. I did not even know this type of connection was a possibility until many years later. There wasn't anyone close to me who could model the life of a person who was surrendered to Christ, but I always knew somehow that the Lord was with me. I can remember thinking about the Lord and even talking to Him. I would try to read my Bible, but I would get discouraged because I didn't understand the Scriptures. Years later, after I fully surrendered my life to the Lord, He opened my heart and made me hungry for the Scriptures and gave me insight and understanding as I read His Word. I saw the Lord would answer many of my prayers. He spared my life many times over the years. God did not allow Satan to have his way when I was born, and God is still keeping me alive to this day. I know my Lord is always with me.

I remember when we would go see Onalee's parents after Dad and she married. Her father was a drinker. Grandpa and Dad would go over and visit a man who lived across the road from them. The three of them would drink tequila together. Usually, on our way home, Dad would not let Mom drive. Because he had been drinking, he imagined that Mom was going to leave him. He would become very angry and threaten to kill us all. He would even threaten to drive the car into a tree. I remember standing in the back behind his seat and crying and pleading with him, "Please Daddy don't kill us." It seemed that every time he got drunk, I would end up pleading with him not to kill us or someone else who had made him mad. It had to be the Lord that let him listen. Not only was my real mother unfaithful to Dad, but that is what he saw happen in his family during his childhood. Dad witnessed that his mother was not faithful to his dad. Because of what he saw in his childhood, Dad could not believe someone could be faithful and honest.

Another time, when I was about 8 years old, we had a boxer dog. I loved that dog, and he was my constant companion. He did something, I can't remember what, and Dad got his rifle and threatened to shoot the dog. I stepped in between the dog and the rifle and told Dad he was going to have to shoot me too. The dog lived and died of natural causes, and I am still here. I know now I am only here because it is the Lord's will. The Lord has really had His hand on me.

I had always loved horses, and the Lord finally answered my prayer to have a horse when I was fifteen years old. Dad and Mom had gotten a place in the country with some land. It made it possible for me to be able to have a horse of my own. From the age of ten I worked any kind of a job I could, saving most of the money I earned. I knew that someday I was going to have a horse. My dad let me have one, but told me if he ever had to spend a dime on it or take care of it, it would be gone. I had the money saved for my first horse, and dad never did spend a dime on her.

Also, at the age of fifteen, I added a part-time job in a store as a cashier to my other two jobs of babysitting and cleaning houses. When I was not in school or working, I was on my horse. Lady and I bonded, and she took care of me. I could get away and find peace when I was riding Lady. I could wander in the woods following the trails, not worrying about getting lost, because when it was time to go back, I would turn Lady around and let her take us home. No matter how many turns we might have made, she always got us back out to the road to go home. I learned to ride on Lady. One time she was galloping across a field. She stumbled in a dip and I fell off. She came back and stood over me trying to figure out what happened to me.

I really did not date much while growing up. It was pretty much school, work and time with my animals. Eventually, though, I met, dated, and married a young man named Ralph. I married Ralph when I was twenty-one years old. Four years later I had our first child, Melissa, when I was twenty-five. Our second child, Rodney, came twenty-one months later. When the kids were little Ralph was diagnosed with Rheumatoid Arthritis. His joints swelled, and the doctor prescribed Gold Salt injections and twenty aspirin a day. The doctors told me that Ralph would be an invalid in a wheelchair, and one day he would need constant care. Hiring a nurse was expensive and not a possibility. I knew I had to plan for Ralph's current medical needs and the future of my family. If I did not want to live on disability and raise a family, I needed to find a job. I also knew it would be best if I could find something I could do in my home. That is when my hairdresser told me I should go to school to be a beautician. She knew I loved hand crafts and that I would probably love doing hair. I went to beauty school and opened a shop in my home where I worked for twenty years. I loved doing hair. Another prayer was answered. I did not want my kids to be cared for by someone else while I worked. I wanted children, and it was especially important that I be the one to raise my children. I would not even leave my children with a babysitter until they had started school. God answered that prayer and gave me my heart's desire. Way out in the country, never advertising my beauty shop, I had as much work as I could physically stand and do in a day. The Lord kept bringing the people to my shop. Some of my customers became almost like family. Some customers came to me the entire twenty years that my shop was open. During this time, I prayed that the Lord would heal Ralph; God did not heal him, but God did allow Ralph to stay well enough to be able to work and move about on his own.

About a year after Ralph had been diagnosed with arthritis, our son, Rodney, was diagnosed with juvenile rheumatoid arthritis. Rodney was six years old. His little joints would swell. Rodney was in so much pain. We were told that he might not live to be an adult. He is now almost fifty years old. Another answered prayer. I have so much to thank the Lord for!

Ralph and I were married for almost eighteen years. When the kids were little, he would attend church with us. After a while, he told me he did not truly think God was real. Later in our marriage Ralph started hanging out with some men from work. His coworkers ran around on their wives and were into pornography. Ralph wanted me to take part in wife swapping and I would have no part of it. Finally, when our daughter Melissa started to become a teen, Ralph didn't think she needed any privacy. I told Ralph, he was wrong and that his thinking was messed up about Melissa needing her own private space. He informed me I was the one who was wrong instead of him. I was unsure of what to do. I found and spoke with a counselor about this situation. After my first visit with the counselor, he wanted to speak with Ralph. The counselor agreed with me that Melissa was at the age where she needed her own privacy. Ralph told us we were both crazy.

Shortly after this incident, Ralph and I attended a marriage encounter weekend and follow-up meetings with several couples. There was no change. The final straw that pushed me to get the divorce was seeing Ralph put some whiskey in his coke one evening. I never tolerated alcohol in the home. I had seen enough of what it can do to people. In my experiences, alcohol makes people do things that they would never do if they were sober. I talked to my pastor and he said I had biblical grounds for a divorce. I prayed about it, asking the Lord what to do. I decided I was not about to put our daughter in harm's way, so I filed for divorce. After we told Melissa that her dad and I were getting divorce, she looked at us and asked, "Who is leaving?" When we told her that her dad was leaving, Missy said, "Good, maybe this house will be happy now." A couple days later when Melissa and I were alone, she told me, "It's okay mom, God will take care of us." And God did. The Lord has never let me down.

After the kids and I were living alone, I met Bob. The kids wanted to take karate classes. I took the kids, but did not want to take classes. I was not too excited about getting kicked or punched. The kids convinced me I needed to take karate because I was home alone working in my beauty shop. Being alone in my shop in the country, I never knew who was going to walk in my back door. Bob was owner and master instructor at the karate school. Bob had been alone for a lot of years. We ended up dating and in time got married. Bob was so good to the kids and me. We had a good life together, although it was too short. I am often reminded that life is about God's plan, not ours. It takes a long and deep walk with our Lord to start getting that into our head and to be okay with all the trials that come into our lives. You must know and believe that He knows what is best for your good and for what will bring Him glory.

2

"YOU ARE GOING TO BE ALONE SOON!"

J had no clue I was about to be plunged into a deeper walk with the Lord. I would be taught the meaning of "Sovereignty of the Lord." He is in control, or the term God is above all things, are not just words written in His Bible for us to read. I was going to learn when He chooses for us to understand the meaning of these terms in our personal lives, we are going to be taken into circumstances that we would never dream we would be in. I was going to start learning to live my life, learning He is Sovereign. Believing God is Sovereign, I have learned, is the key Satan wants to keep from us. As long as Satan can keep people believing that things just randomly happen in life, he can keep us from having the peace that only our Lord can give us. As long as Satan is in control, people will be blinded. It is not just the unbeliever who is blinded but those who think that once they are saved, they are fine. There are many people sitting in the church pews in our day, who do not get into God's word to learn the truth, who are just as blind. They may be saved but have not gone on to sanctification. We are saved first then we must go on to sanctification, growing in our walk with the Lord. Many believe once they are saved that is all there is to the Christian life. Salvation is only the beginning of a new, transformed life. Sanctification involves growing in our walk with our Lord. I have heard it said that if we are not closer to the Lord now than we were a few years ago, we need to stop and check ourselves. We need to ask Jesus to let us see ourselves as He sees us. If we have left the path that the Lord had us on, we need to repent and ask Him to get us back on the right path.

Some people get really mad at me when I talk about God's complete control over all He has created. (*2 Chronicles 20:6, He said: Lord, God of our ancestors, are you not the God who is in heaven, and do you not rule over all the kingdoms of the nations? Power and might are in Your hand, and no one can stand against you. CSB*). Now when I read scripture like this, it gets me excited to think we do have a God such as this. He has not given us His power. That is why we have to die out to self. He wants to put His power through us. He wants to grow us into vessels for His use and glory, not for what we want.

When the Lord wants to pour out His saving grace upon a person or work on a person in anyway, I have learned, God will burden a committed believer to pray for that person or situation. I have learned there are requirements that have to be met for God to answer prayer. God works through prayer, but people often do not realize it is His prayer through us that He will answer. When the person whom He calls to pray begins to pray through the power of the Holy Spirit, then God will hear his prayer and send the Holy Spirit to work on that person's heart. I am not talking about praying in tongues. I have always understood every word I have ever prayed. I have not always understood why I was praying what I felt directed to pray. It might take some time before the Lord would reveal to me why I prayed the way I was being directed to pray.

Though it took many hard trials, and I know there are still many more to come should the Lord leave me here on earth a while longer, I will praise His holy name. I was one whom He chose. God put it upon the hearts of those godly people to pray for me. I had no idea my world, as I knew it, was going to take a drastic change soon.

"You are going to be alone soon." What a strange thought. I was out very early in the morning carrying a load of hay across my back yard when this thought came across my mind. I had a couple of lamas, angora goats, a donkey I had adopted that came from out west, and my daughter Missy and I had riding horses. We also raised miniature horses. All these animals were divided off in separate pastures according to stallions, mares, weanlings and mares with new foals, and etc. I was out doing morning chores before having to go in and get cleaned up to start doing hair in my beauty salon. I was blessed that my salon was there in my home. I thought again, "What a strange thought," and proceeded with my chores and the busy day I knew I had ahead of me in the salon.

The very next morning same time, same place, I heard it again; it was a voice I could hear in my head telling me, "You are going to be alone soon!" "Okay," I started thinking, I have heard this voice before. It had been a very long time since I had heard this His voice; I better pay attention. All day it was on my mind, and when my daughter Missy came home from work that evening, I decided to share what I heard the morning before and that morning. After talking about what I heard, we said nothing to anyone else. My daughter believed me, but we knew no one else would.

You see people had been telling me for years that the Lord does not speak to us in a voice we can hear. Well, I had heard the Lord speak to me a few times before. It does not matter how many people tell me the Lord does not talk to us in this way. I know because I have lived and experienced hearing Him. The Holy Spirit talks to me and I hear Him in many ways. I was beginning to understand that when God speaks to me, there is going to be something difficult ahead for me to go through.

Knowing something may be coming, does not make it any easier to go through, whatever it may be, but knowing He is with me, gives me something to hold on to. I was not journaling these encounters at this time in my life. The Lord would speak to me about journaling about what I saw Him doing in my life a few years later.

This was late fall when I heard the Lord speak to me. Missy and I would talk about it every now and then. We felt it had something to do with my husband, Bob. Missy was dating a young man, and they were talking about getting married, which would mean she would be leaving home. Even though my children would be out of our home, Bob would still be there with me. My son, Rod, was already gone living not far away.

In November, Bob, my husband, and I had a trip planned through the Midland Community Center to go to Branson, Missouri for a few days on a bus trip. We had some friends going, and they wanted us to go with them. Bob was an electrician by trade and had worked with Mable's husband, and I had done Mable's hair for years. We loved to travel, so we decided it would be a fun trip to take with them. Little did I realize it would be my last trip ever to take with Bob.

Bob had competed in weight lifting when he was younger, and that caused him to need his hip joints replaced. He was due to have his second hip replacement the first of January, so we thought we would take this trip with our friends before he would have to be down for a while.

We went on the trip, and we had a wonderful time. I had kind of lost track of what I had heard the Lord say to me a couple of months earlier, because everything seemed to be going so well. It came time for him to have his surgery; all went well with the surgery except he had a little trouble coming out of the anesthesia. The next morning, I was getting ready to go to the hospital. I got a call from a nurse at the hospital telling me to please get there as soon as possible. Bob was determined he was going to get up and out of the hospital.

You see, my husband was a high-ranking black belt in several styles of the Martial Arts. He had a school in the area for many years, and everyone knew him. The nurses were thinking they needed to restrain him, but they did not know how that was going to happen without someone getting hurt. This was not like my husband at all. I hurried and got out to the hospital as fast as I could. As soon as I walked into the room and started talking to him, he settled down. No one could figure out why his mood changed all of a sudden. The first hip replacement went fine with no complications. The rest of the few days Bob had to stay in the hospital, I stayed right there with him leaving only to go home shower and change clothes.

Finally, we got to go home, but I started noticing little things that were different. The TV had to be louder and louder for him to hear it and he would ask me to repeat things over and over again. He was still using a walker a couple of weeks after getting out of the hospital One day he called me into the bathroom where he was and I could not believe my eyes. Blood was everywhere. He had a massive nosebleed. I grabbed a bath towel and got him into the car. He was not walking well, bleeding from the nose in gushes, and I had steps to get him down. I got him into the car. I drove as fast as I could hoping a policeman would stop me and help me get him to the hospital without delays. All I can say is the Lord had the way cleared for us. I had a lot of traffic lights to go through, and they were green. In the emergency room a doctor packed his nose, and told us he needed to go to a specialist. The emergency room nurses got us in to see an ears, nose and throat specialist the next day. I was able to take Bob back home that night.

The Lord was walking with me through each moment, I can see as I look back. I called my parents to tell them what happened. My parents insisted that they should go with me to take my husband to the specialist the next day. I really did not want to leave him alone even for a moment to go and park the car, so I was glad they wanted to go help me. The packing, the doctor put in Bob's nose the night before in the emergency room to stop the flow of blood, was still holding. I knew from the amount of blood in the bathroom and on the bath towel that Bob had lost a tremendous amount of blood. He was not stable from his hip replacement, and the amount of blood he had lost made him weak.

I went in the exam room with my husband and the doctor. I started telling him what I had been seeing happening with my husband and what had happened with the massive nose bleed the night before. After looking into my husband's eyes, the doctor looked at me, went to the door and told one of the nurses standing by the desk he wanted an x-ray of this man's head, stat. The stat part set me on edge. The nurse brought a wheel chair, and the doctor never left my husband's side as he was taken to x-ray and brought back to me. The doctor told me my husband was scheduled the next morning for a biopsy. There was something there, and a biopsy was needed quickly.

The next morning the Lord knew I was going to need more support, and, thank the Lord, Missy and my parents went to the hospital with us. I was told what would happen in the procedure. After the biopsy my husband would sleep for a little bit, but I would be able to take him home when he woke up. My family and I were in the waiting room when the doctor came in to talk to us. The look on his face almost made my heart stop. He sat down in front of me and started telling me what he had just seen in my husband's head. A massive tumor that had already eaten the front lobe of Bob's brain, was starting to push his eyes out and was from ear to ear, which was why he was not hearing well. It was huge and a fast-growing tumor that was eating him up by the day.

The next thing I remember was the doctor turning to the nurse standing behind him and saying, "Oh no, she is going into shock." I started shaking uncontrollably. I was turning so cold, and my mind was going blank. They rushed to get warm blankets to wrap me in, and they gave me something to try to get me to drink. I remember them telling me, "You have to come out of this, your husband is going to be waking up soon and he will need you to be strong for him. He is really going to need you." Thank the Lord, my family was there. Thank the Lord, He did pull me together and helped me stand in His strength for what was ahead. Bob was put in the hospital right away. We were told that surgery to remove the tumor was impossible. Surgery was scheduled as soon as possible because shunts had to be put in Bob's head and chest for chemo shots, and a line needed to be put in for five days of chemo treatments right away. We were told this was a very aggressive tumor and it had to be treated quickly. A few days after entering the hospital my husband did not know anyone but me. He did not know what was going on, or where he was. My husband was not a Christian, but as long as I was beside of him, Bob was at peace and calm. It had to be the Lord bringing this peace to my husband.

I stayed by his side night and day. It was a hard thing to watch, Not only was the tumor eating Bob's brain, but they were giving him a combination of two chemo medicines. What they gave Bob was destroying not only the tumor, but everywhere in his body that had fast growing cells. As it was explained to me the chemo would destroy any fast-growing cells in the body. I was not to worry, once the tumor was destroyed, they would fix up the damage that the chemo had done in the rest of the body. This was my first experience with cancer and chemo treatments.

I stayed by Bob's side night and day. When I went home to shower, some of the guys from Bob's karate school would take turns staying with him for me. Even though Bob had known and had these guys in his karate classes since they were kids, he did not know them now. He was always so happy when I got back to be with him. Bob made it through his first session of treatments and was able to come home for a few days. It was so good to be home. He had not really healed from the hip surgery, and the chemo and all he had going on in his body did not help with his healing. The chemo was destroying the tissue in Bob's mouth, and it was so hard for him to eat. When we were in the hospital his mouth bled a lot. He had lost so much weight and I was trying to get calories down him. I made him a lot of protein drinks loaded with ice-cream and anything else I thought he could get down. Before we knew, it was time to take Bob back for his second session of chemo.

After three days of chemo, in the evening, Bob seemed to be struggling, and I got up to swab blood out of his mouth. As I reached up toward his face, his hands came up and he gently took hold of my wrists to stop me. A nurse walked into the room just then and saw what was happening. Bob was dying. Just as God had told me those two mornings in the fall, I would be alone soon.

The doctors kept telling me that he was going to make it. I was told he could live fine without the front lobe of his brain. The front lobe of the brain was what controlled a person's emotions, but other than that he should be fine. A few months later, after my husband passed, a nurse, who had worked on the floor Bob was on, decided to come and tell me what really happened. She knew who I was from my beauty shop. She told me the doctors knew all along that he would not make it. She told me he was going to die no matter what. If he had not had the chemo, he would have drifted off into a coma and died without all the pain he had to suffer. The doctors wanted to experiment and see what the combination of these two chemo medicines given at the same time would do with such a fast-growing tumor. I remember the time Bob was home between the treatments. They had me take Bob to a brain specialist in Detroit, Michigan, a three-hour drive from our home. They wanted this doctor to examine Bob and look at all of Bob's x-rays. This was not going to be an easy task as weak as my husband was. With his hip still not healed, riding that far was not going to be easy for him. It was going to take much of a day to go there and back. My parents were able to go with me to help me. There was no way I could have handled this on my own. The doctor examined Bob and told me the same thing the other doctors had told me. I remember praying, "God help me."

I was stressed, but still there was a calm I could not explain. Bob was not the only one to lose weight. The nurses insisted I eat Bob's meals he could not eat. We had to pay for them, so they told me I needed to eat them. I still got down to 89 pounds. God had spoken to me in October; we made the trip to Brandon, Missouri in November; the hip surgery was in January; the nose-bleed started the first of February, and he was gone the first of April.

What did I learn? When God speaks, it is going to happen; He is sovereign. He makes the plans for our lives; we don't. I was made aware in real life that God had a hand on my life all along, and I was going to be allowed to see the reality of *(Proverbs 16:9 A person's heart plans his way, but the Lord determines his steps. CSB)*. I was just beginning to be made aware these were not just words written on the pages in the Bible. I was going to see this worked out in my life. I had it in my head; I knew what I had read. Now I was being taken through the process of getting it from my head to my heart. The people in the Bible serve as examples for us to learn that God works in our lives in our day just as He did in their lives long ago.

In a few days after the funeral, I went to the hospital to see what the bill was going to be. I thought for sure I was going to have to sell our little farm to pay the hospital and doctors' bills. I sat there as they were running off the paper that kept stacking up on the floor by the printer as everything was being tallied up. The more paper that was stacking up on the floor, the more my heart sank. I thought, "Oh Lord, what is going to happen? Where will I get the money for all these bills?"

I went home and started praying asking the Lord, "What am I going to do?" With all the stress of what I had gone through, I had forgotten that my husband, the year before, decided to take out a cancer policy on himself. Between my husband's work insurance and the cancer policy, all the bills were paid. We had bought a car, and he had put insurance on the car should anything happen to him; it was paid for. I know this was the hand of the Lord taking care of me, knowing what was going to happen. He had prepared for me ahead of time what I had no idea was coming. *(Phil. 4:19. And my God will supply all your needs according to His riches in glory in Christ Jesus. CSB).* We had no clue when Bob took that extra cancer insurance policy out on himself that in just a few months over a year he would be gone.

I know me, and if the Lord had not let me know He was in control, I would have been angry and bitter because of what happened. The grief of losing Bob was enough to handle without adding more on my emotions. I know it was God's great love and His compassion and mercy upon me that let me realize that He was in this and preparing me for what was coming.

When I look back at what I learned from all this, what seemed to be the end of my life was really the beginning of a new and deeper walk with the Lord. I had been saved when I was eleven years old, and I was walking in all the light I had at the time for all those years. I was forty-eight years old when Bob died, and little did I dream that the Lord had a much deeper walk with Him planned for my life. He had spoken to me a few times, and I knew His voice, but what He was really after was a fully surrendered life. I had some patrons in my beauty shop with whom I had gone to church, and I had done their hair for years. They became concerned for me and started praying for me when they realized the situation with my husband. I believe the Lord gave them the discernment to know I was going to be alone. They told me later they were concerned for me and what was going to happen to me. I knew enough about the Bible stories, about how the Lord took Moses, Paul and even our Lord Jesus into the wilderness to be tested and to grow them spiritually. I did not know my walk into the wilderness with the Lord was about to begin. God knew what it was going to take to get me where He wanted me. My kids were ready to move off on their own walk in life. I did not feel like I was really needed.

I was used to doing everything with Bob. He enjoyed the animals and went to horse shows when Missy and I went to show the minis. I trained with him in the martial arts, as well as, attending all of his martial arts events. We did everything together; we even went grocery shopping together. About eight months after his death, I was really emotionally going down. My kids were busy doing their own thing, and my husband was gone. I kept busy in the beauty shop, with the animals and farm, even repainted the whole house inside. With all that I was doing to try to keep busy, I felt I had no purpose for my life anymore. I did not really want to do anything, but drove myself to keep busy to pass time.

One night, I will never forget I got up at 2:00 a.m. and fell flat out on my face on my bedroom floor. I told the Lord I did not want this life anymore. I begged Him to take me; I did not want this life anymore, and He could have it. I really wanted him to take my life. I stood in enough light to know I could not take my own life, so I had to ask Him to take it. He could take me to be with Him, or He could take this life and do whatever He wanted to with it. Well, I am seventy-five years old. He took me up on the offer, and we know which way He chose to take me.

I had entered a world I had not heard anyone ever talk about. In church I had not heard any testimonies from people who had a close walk with the Lord. At this point I had not read any Christian books. I read my Bible some. I had never heard any Christians talk about dying to self nor had I ever heard any pastors speak of it. I did not know that when I got down on my knees and surrendered my life to the Lord, I was going to enter a dark cloud with the Lord that was going to take me on a path that would lead me closer to Jesus each day. I had no clue I was going to be plunged into this demon-possessed valley that would lead me closer to Jesus and put me in the furnace of affliction to burn the dross off of me, and make me look more like Jesus. I did not know Jesus did not want to take my life, but His purpose was that the self within me was going to be destroyed so that He could, through the Holy Spirit, live His life on earth again through me. What I was going to learn was that all those chains Satan had me bound up in for all those years were going to slowly, one by one, be cut loose and drop off of me the longer I walked with my Lord. I felt hatred, fear, and jealousy. We think this is the normal way of life until the Lord gets ahold of us and starts setting us free. I was going to be taken into a dark cloud, but it was going to make me cling to my Lord. God had me in His grip and was holding me tight. He would be walking me toward the light, but I did not know this then. (I can see as I look back, I would have slipped off the path He had me on, had the Lord not had a tight grip on me.)

There is a saying, "I wouldn't take anything for my journey now." My life had consisted of many heart aches and tragedies up to this point. the difference now was that I was on a new path, and I was going to get to see more of Jesus in my life, and, learn how much He is in control. I wouldn't take anything for my journey now because I can see where it has taken me. I hear people say, "I wish I could go back to my younger years." I have a glimpse of what is ahead waiting for those who stay close to the Lord, and I would not want to walk one day back. I am keeping my eyes looking forward.

I still have lots to learn, but I plan on scooping up all those that the Lord will bring across my path. I pray He will use me to reach out to help them learn and walk along this path to freedom with Jesus. I am learning, and it would have a dedicated Christian to sit down with a Bible and talk to me about the things of the Lord. I needed someone to explain how Jesus works in our lives, and what He expects of us. I was going to learn: God's ways are not our ways. He knows exactly what it is going to take for us to learn, and He engineers the circumstances to teach us.

3

STILL HERE

So, I have surrendered my life to my Lord; He did not take me home to be with Him as I was still alive. So, what next? When I think back, I was saved when I was eleven years old. I remembered the preacher saying that when a person was saved his/her life would change. I do not remember the preacher telling us exactly any details of what those changes would be. I remember him preaching about us going to hell, and how we would suffer if we did not get right with the Lord. I looked for changes to come within myself immediately, but there did not seem to be any changes that I noticed. I did not know what to expect. I had just heard, "The Lord will change your life." I loved Jesus as much as I knew how. I understood I would not please Him if I used His name in vain, drank, stole from others and all those obvious wrongs. But I always felt there was something still missing. As most of my family did not know the Lord, I did not know where to turn. The pastor I was saved under seemed to focus on preaching hell fire and brimstone sermons, which we need to hear. What I thought later was that he was trying to scare people into heaven. We need to hear about hell, and we do not hear enough about it these days. In our days we are hearing about God's love and nothing about God's wrath or judgment that will come upon those who do not obey His commandments. But we need to hear the whole truth, not just bits and pieces. What some are preaching today is known as the social gospel.

After surrendering my life to the Lord, I did start feeling changes coming, like a deep desire to study my Bible. I started reading a little more in my Bible. I began reading books of the Bible instead of a story here or there. As I was reading and absorbing His Word, the Lord started pointing out some of my behaviors that had to go. The Lord had gifted me with a love for animals, not people. I had a deep hate in my heart for some people who had done or said things to hurt me or my parents, but I loved animals. The more time I spent with the Lord I could feel a change coming in my heart toward people. From early childhood on, I only felt safe with my animals. I noticed changes coming in my heart that I had never felt before. I had a lot of issues that needed to be cleaned out. I feared so many things: getting lost in an unfamiliar area by myself, speaking out even in a small group of people, not having enough food and starving to death. I was a mess and did not realize where I needed the changes made until after He started making changes in me. This is something I had never been aware of before. When the Lord started making the changes, I could tell the difference in myself. Something I always was aware of though was that my Lord has had His hand on me. He has spoken to me, and I have always known it was He. I have seen Him move in situations that only He could have been in, and only God could have worked out. I took it for granted this was how the Lord interacted with everyone who went to church. When I started attending church on a regular basis, I was in for a shock. Not everyone who attends church is truly God's child. I had a lot to learn.

I could feel a softening that I never believed could be in my heart towards people who had rejected me. You see my birth mother did not want me. She would have aborted me but my dad had threatened her. So many situations in my life caused me to feel unwanted. One was that I was a product of a divorce. I felt like an outcast even in my dad's family. Living with my grandparents, I knew my grandpa loved me, but I could tell my grandma only tolerated me. My cousins got treated differently than I did.

I saw a lot of hate displayed in my family as I was growing up. There were several family members on my dad's side who drank a lot, and some would get really mean when they drank. My birth mother was pretty much out of my life until I was in my later teens. My birth mother, too, was a heavy drinker. I believe she drank to forget all she had done. The drinking did not help her forget; it would only make her life worse. Mom was a closet drinker. She would only drink when she did not have to work. Her work place would have never dreamed she drank. She was a dedicated worker and a generous giver to those who needed help. My father only drank occasionally, when I was little, but had a bad temper. Eventually dad stopped drinking, but the temper carried on for most of his life.

I had gotten so I hated having to be around people who were drinking because of all the awful things that would happen. It seemed we did not go to a wedding that fights would not break out when there was drinking involved. I had made up my mind I was never going to drink. I wanted to know at all times what I was doing. I was not going to let alcohol take my life over. I had gotten very bitter toward people who drank or used drugs. My attitude towards them was they were worth nothing. I had no compassion for people who would drink, especially those who drank until they had lost all control of themselves. My attitude was if a drunk fell down in front of me, I would step over him and kick him as I went. This was an area the Lord started working on soon after my surrender to Him.

It was to take a lot of years to soften this hard heart and clean the hatred out completely. It seemed He started softening my heart with people more distant to me. Later He started bringing into my life those closer up. God is so good; He knows what we can handle, and He does not push us hard, but gently leads us along the path to restoration. I remember there were two people brought in my life just about the same time. Not too long after I had surrendered my life to the Lord on my bedroom floor and cried out to Jesus to take me, I soon found out Satan does go to church. Yes, these people the Lord first brought into my life to start softening my heart went to church. One would get high on her pain pills, and the other drank until she could not walk. One would call me from a phone booth (no cell phones back then) because she had taken a hand full of pain pills. She would end up going out in her car, and when the pills would kick in, and she would get lost and call me to come get her. I would have to have her try to describe a store or gas station where the phone booth was that she was calling me from. Or she would call me from her home telling she was going to kill herself. She had tried to kill herself and had been hospitalized for slitting her wrists. Another time she drove her car head on into a row of parked cars, so I knew she was serious about killing herself. She lived in an apartment by herself but did these things when her parents were out of town. As a matter of fact, her father was the pastor of the church we were attending. There was a spirit in this woman that was not of the Lord. What amazed me was that I cared and really wanted to help her.

Because I was learning that the Lord is in control over every situation that comes into our lives, He was letting me see how Satan works in people. With my family and twenty years of working with people in my beauty shop, I had learned a lot, but God was opening my eyes to discern at a deeper level. It was kind of scary. The looks I would get at times or comments that were made to me from certain people, was like Satan knew that I could see him working in these people. It was like Satan was toying with me. Back at this time, I had no clue that one day I would be standing in front of a group of ladies giving a presentation at a women's retreat entitled. "Do You Know Your Adversary?" The Lord was not only teaching me about Himself, but He was letting me see with His eyes how Satan works in the lives of people under Satan's control.

The other person that the Lord brought would get drunk in a bar and would call to tell me, "I can't get myself home." Most of the time a bartender would have to take the phone and tell me where the bar was. I did not know where most of the bars were. My thought was to blow them all up, not go in them. My son lived close by, so I would call him, and he would come and help me get this person home. If my daughter was at home, she would go with me.

One night going to the bar to pick up this person with my son. This person drank until he could not pick up another glass; in essence, his intent was to drink himself to death. My son and I drove into the parking lot of the bar; we saw a body lying in the parking lot. We drove up to him and showed our head lights on him to see who it was. We recognized the person. It was the guy we were there to get. We did not know if he was alive or dead. We jumped out of my car and ran up to see what condition he was in. We saw he had passed out. When I bent over to help my son pick this person up, it flashed before my mind what I had said for years. "There was no drunk worth bending over and picking up." Here I was with Rod in the middle of a bar parking lot, late at night picking up, a person passed out from drinking. That was a real God movement in my heart. I have learned not to say I am not going to do something. God can and does engineer circumstances to make us do that very thing when He is starting His life-transforming work in our hearts and minds. I was learning to have compassion for people that I had never before had in my heart.

There was another young man in the church who became so depressed that he tried to kill himself by jumping off the bridge in our town. He missed the water and landed on a pile of rocks. He broke every bone just about in his body. He lived, but was a mess for a long time. A couple of us would go to visit him and take-home cooked food for him to eat.

Something I did notice was that no matter how bad a shape these first two people were in, they always knew me and my phone number. Even though they knew my son well, when he was with me at the time of these encounters, it was like Rod was not there. One time my son and his girlfriend were at the house when I got a call, so they both went with me. When we got the person back to his apartment, I was trying to get this person to eat hoping to sober him up before we left him alone. My son and his girlfriend were sitting at the kitchen table and this person walked up to me and asked me, "Is there anyone else here with us?"

It has been strange how people have seemed to know me when they did not know anyone else. When Bob was taking chemo treatments before He died, he always knew me when he knew no one else. These two people I was just telling about knew me when they did not seem to be aware of others around them. I had a lady whose hair I did in my beauty salon for a few years. Anita had slipped into dementia. She did not know her husband and family but always knew me. Her husband would tell me she would call to make her appointments with me each week to get her hair done, and she could not make any other phone calls. While I was doing her hair, she would tell me all about that strange man living in her house. She was worried about what her husband would think if he came home and found a strange man in their home and in the same bed with her. When her hair was done, she would not want to go get in the car with him to go home. I had to take her out and tell her it was okay for her to go with her husband. Anita would tell me that at times she would see Jesus, and He would tell her everything was going to be alright.

I can look back now and see that the Lord was using many of those patrons of my beauty shop to soften my heart. Some of these people had been my customers for the twenty years I had my shop. It was like the Lord was letting me see people below the surface. I walked through a lot of joy and heartaches with these people the Lord brought to me. I knew the Lord brought them. I lived out in the country and all I did was put a sign out front of our place after I had completed schooling and apprenticeship. I did no advertising of any kind. I was not that great of a hair dresser, but the Lord made me a good listener. I was so busy that most days I did chores in the morning darkness and after dark in the evening. God blessed me with hurting people so that He could show compassion through me to them. Me of all people.

4

HIS PLANS, NOT MINE

This may be a good time to stop and tell you a little about my experience with the Holy Spirit's working in my life. I was being taught as a young child of God that God is real. He works supernaturally in our lives. For some reason He has chosen to show me, to believe first, and after believing, He would let me see, in detail, how He is I in control of my life. Many people do not believe me; most people think that we are in control of our lives. Because God has shown me that He is sovereign through circumstances I have experienced, He has let me see Him work in supernatural ways. God engineers our circumstances in whatever way He wants, so that it works out for His glory. Sometimes it may be through blessings, but most of the time the blessings come after a hard trial. There have not been many times that He has not let me see why He allowed me to go through a hard trial and what His purpose was. It may have taken a little while or a few years, but He lets me see

His purpose. Sometimes His purpose is to use me, other times to teach me something, or other times to let me see Him. All of the circumstances have been engineered to praise Him for what a Mighty God He is.

In time God allowed me to see that He removed my husband out of my life because He was going to move me into a deeper spiritual walk with Him. He had other plans for my life. I would not have a man to lean on anymore, only God. Oh yes, He was going to bring a man, but no matter how much I wanted to lean on him, the Lord knew I was never going to be able to. God wanted to be the Rock I was to lean on.

For me who never planned on leaving my children, family, beauty shop, farm or hometown, I was soon to learn the Lord had other plans for my life. In time the Lord brought another man into my life. This person was my daughter's boss, and he started bringing his little boy with him to the farm. He knew, Missy and I were taking care of the farm while working at our jobs. We worked until late hours in the night doing all that needed to be done to keep the little farm up. He and his wife were divorced, and he thought it would be a good idea to bring his son and help Missy and me on the farm. His son could enjoy being around all the animals. He had grown up on a farm and loved it but now lived in an apartment. Rod helped us some, but we sure could use this man's and he said he expected no pay for the work. I loved to cook, so figured he and his son could join us for a meal on the days they were there.

He had asked Missy at work one day to ask me if it would be okay if they came. Missy and I talked, and she shared with me a little about him. He worked an outside job as well as pastoring a church. His wife was running out on him, and because of all the stress in his life, he was told it would be better if he stepped away from the ministry until he could get his life settled down again.

I had told the Lord that I was fine by myself. I was learning that the Lord would care for me. I had made the Lord my husband in my heart. But He was in control of my life, so if there was anyone that He wanted in my life, the Lord would have to bring him to my back door. I don't know why I told the Lord this, but I remember talking to Him and saying this. People always came in a side door by the drive way, when they came to visit. The back-door lead to the barn. When this person came the first time, he followed Missy home from work, and she always parked back by the barn. When they were walking up to the back door, I heard that voice again speaking to me, as I was walking out my back door to see them. I heard the same voice that told me I was going to be alone soon, say, "I want him back. Can I use you?" I knew that voice. Same voice, not telling me this time something, but this time asking me to do something. I said, "Yes, Lord." I was not going to say "No" to God. He does not give details either, to what you are saying yes to. He is God. In my mind he was someone else to help.

I had all kinds of animals on the farm, and kids like animals. I always enjoyed having kids around and sharing my animals with them. I thought this guy's son would enjoy the animals, and it would be good for him to spend time on a farm instead of sitting in an apartment when he was with his dad. The neighbor kids would be there a lot.

When I had puppies, a little neighbor boy would come to the door and ask if the puppies could come out to play. I would put them in a laundry basket, and he would love to sit in the back yard and play with the puppies. When he was done playing, he would come tell me and help me get the puppies back in the house again. We were always having baby animals being born, and the kids loved being able to come see and pet the babies.

In time Missy's boss and I started dating. He was raised up and pastored in the Nazarene denomination. I had not ever attended that denomination and knew nothing about it. My step mom told me she had attended a Nazarene church before she married my dad and they believed a lot like us. I started attending church with him. About a year after we started dating, we became engaged, and we got married.

Our plans were to stay on the farm as he loved the horses and all the animals that were there. Missy and I loved to trail ride and camp with our horses. We would go on these trail rides and camp with a horse club I had belonged to for years. With Missy, we would go to horse shows to show the miniature horses and lamas. We planned on raising horses and lamas; we cut and baled our own hay for our animals and sold some. We thought life would go this way forever.

With encouragement and talking with the pastor at the Nazarene church we were attending, my husband took some classes to get back in the ministry to be ordained. When my husband was in the ministry before he had taken classes to be licensed, but not ordained. He had a church when he was advised to step away until things in his life settled down again.

It had crossed my mind that the Lord intended Missy's boss to be back in the ministry again (*The memory came back to my mind when the Lord spoke to me while I was watching Missy's boss and Missy come toward the house the first day he came. I kind of thought I was there to encourage him on as I had seen God do thorough me with others.*) I did not know I was going to be part of this plan when the Lord spoke to me. I would have never in my life dreamed I would be a pastor's wife one day. I did a lot of pastor's wives' hair over the years, but never thought I would walk in those shoes. It never occurred to me to want to. I had my farm and animals, ministry moved people; I was not moving.

When he had completed the classes, he needed to get a church, we were at our local fairgrounds showing some of our miniature horses. We had taken our camper to stay out on the grounds, because we did not want to leave our animals unattended. The church board had a meeting one evening the week of the fair, and several of the guys came to the fairgrounds after the meeting to tell my husband that they had voted him as an Associate Pastor of the church. This was perfect. We were right there in our hometown. I could work in my beauty shop, and still be with our family and on the farm.

God had His plans, and I was soon to realize they started long before He took Bob out of my life. Bob and I had bought a few acres about ten miles from us. Missy and I could haul our horses to this property and ride. There was not any open land to ride our horses on where we lived. All we had was paved, busy roads. The place had a big barn on it, but the house had burned down. We moved our camper to this property and made it our get-away. This is where we met Marc, my now son-in-law. We had heard Marc baled hay for people in the area, and we were given his phone number. Bob and I met Marc at the property to see if he would bale up the hay growing on the place for our horses. Marc drove in and this 6 '5" young man got out of his truck and walked over toward Bob and me. It was like the Lord told me this would be Missy's husband. Missy had not dated much. She was not interested. She loved horses and farm life, and the right one had not come along yet.

When Bob and I got home, and Missy had gotten home from work, I told her, "I met the guy you are going to marry. I believe the Lord let me know." She said, "Mom he probably has a girlfriend." I told her it didn't matter, If this was God speaking, Marc was going to be her husband.

Before the hay all got put in the barn that year, Marc and Missy were dating. Marc was a farmer and raised pretty much all of the feed that He fed his livestock. Missy and Marc both loved farm life. Missy loved to work with the animals and learned to run the farm equipment to help Marc work in the fields. Marc and Missy dated a few years before they got married. Sadly, Bob passed before they married.

The Lord was working again. Just before the kids got married the one hundred acres adjoining Marc's father's property became available for sale. This property was across the road form the acreage Bob and I had purchased. The kids were able to purchase the hundred acres and get a trailer moved in and set up so that when they got married, they could move in. What the Lord told me the first day Bob and I met Marc happened just as He said. Marc and Missy got married in the same year as my husband and I did.

About a year after Marc and Missy got married, my husband got called to a church about forty-five minutes away from where we lived. This was another example of God speaking and leading me into something difficult. I knew the Lord was in it. I was going to have to leave my kids and family, my business, the farm and all the animals. God had called us to a small church. We would be moving into an apartment attached to the church. The little farm where we lived had to be put up for sale. My plans were to continue to drive back each day and work in my shop until the farm and salon sold.

We had moved the animals we had to the farm across from Marc and Missy's until they could be sold. Missy could go across the road and take care of the animals. My plans were not the Lord's plans. I saw my plans fading, but I did not realize how quickly my plans were going to be smashed to pieces. It was turning cold weather and freezing when we hauled the last load of our household goods to move into the church parsonage. Because I trained in the martial arts, I had learned how to fall so the body would not get broken. Carrying the last box in from the car, I slipped on a tiny patch of ice and broke my right wrist. Several bones had broken in that area. I ended up spending some time in the emergency room that night.

I thought I was going to keep my shop open until it was sold. Wrong. The Lord had other plans, and He was going to have His way. I was told that the way my wrist was broken would require wearing a cast for a couple of weeks. I was told that I might have to have surgery if my wrist did not heal correctly. I was told I would need six weeks of therapy after the cast was off to get use of my hand again. Not only was my wrist shattered, but my plans of keeping my business going for a while longer were wiped out.

I would try to start unpacking and doing what I could left-handed. Every time I put my broken wrist down a little bit it would start swelling in the cast. My wrist would start throbbing so bad, I finally decided to get in the lazy boy with a lot of pillows to keep my arm propped up high and read my Bible from cover to cover. I had never read it straight through before. I thought this would be a good time to start. I had lots of time. I sure couldn't do much else.

The third day living in our apartment I was home alone when I heard a knock at the door. I went to the door, and there stood a man I had not seen when we met the people from the church. I could see a woman in the car behind him. They were in their fifties. He asked me if I was the pastor's wife, and I told him I was. He said, "Good," and went to get his wife from the car. He shoved her in the door and said, "She used to go to this church years ago. She keeps wanting to kill herself. I have had her to doctors. I am Catholic and they haven't helped her, I have taken her to other churches in the area. Here, you talk to her." I invited them both in. He said, "No I will sit in the car; you talk to her." As I took her to a chair, I thought, "Lord, I need you here." The Lord did talk to her through me a couple of hours. I cannot tell you what all was said, but it was the Lord speaking though me. I remember thinking I would have never thought to talk to her as He was doing through me. I asked them to come back that evening when my husband was home so they could meet him. God was in it; she never tried to commit suicide again as long as we knew them. Both of them started attending church with us. The next day in my prayer time, the Lord spoke to me and said, "You have to be here." I stopped fussing at God for turning our plans upside down and for my broken wrist.

5

NEW PATH

J did start to read my Bible starting from Genesis 1:1 straight through to the end. I was becoming hungry for more of His word and Him. I was spending a lot of time talking to my Lord. It crossed my mind when I opened that Bible to ask the Lord to teach me. I had read the scripture, *(Psalms 86:11, Teach me your way, Lord, and I will live by Your truth. Give me an undivided mind to fear your name. CSB)*. I wrote it down and began praying this Psalm. It came to mind that He was the One Who is the author of the book I was starting to read. Who would be better to teach me the truths that He wanted me to learn, but the Lord Himself? His word was telling me to ask Him to teach me. He was not only teaching me; He was in control of all things and circumstances. Through reading His Word, I was beginning to see changes in me.

It was not long when the women of the church came to me and wanted me to have a Bible study for them. Oh, my goodness! Some of these ladies had been in the church for years. I told them they needed to be teaching me. They would not take no for an answer. This was really going to stretch my spiritual growth; I soon began to learn. The Lord started putting the old Holiness writer's books into my hands like A. B Simpson, A. W. Tozer, Charles Spurgeon, Oswald Chambers, and E. M. Bounds. A lady who was a retired missionary gave me a devotional, "Streams in the Desert," sharing with me that the Lord let her know I needed this book. He also placed "My Utmost for His Highest" and "Experiencing God" devotionals in my hands to read and I have not stopped reading my Bible to this day, I have read these devotionals every day along with my Bible. I had asked Him to teach me, and He did through these men and woman of God who taught the truths with no compromise. The Lord put in my hands what I was going to need for the rest of my life to keep me moving forward and not run from the trials that were going to come to refine me. The more I studied, the more I wanted. I finally agreed and started a Bible study. I learned to love teaching all the wonderful things I was learning about my Lord. My excitement seemed to get the ladies excited about reading and studying their Bibles; some of them shared with me that they had started reading their Bible from the beginning for the first time.

I had read in *"Streams in the Desert-Oct 3: Therefore, if you desire to know God's voice, never consider final outcome or the possible results, Obey Him even when He asks you to move while you still see only darkness, for He Himself will be a glorious light within you. Then there will quickly spring up within your heart a knowledge of God and a fellowship with Him, which will be overpowering enough in themselves* to hold you and Him together, even in the most sever tests and under the strongest pressures of life." This jumped off the page at me, and it stays in my mind, as a beacon in the dark. Reading year after year from these devotionals I was being led to hang on no matter what. It is through suffering that some of Gods divine truths can be learned. If we are going to develop Christ's character in us, we are going to have to go to the cross. I had given Him my life; I was going to see what He was going to do with it.

My husband and I had not been in this church for long when he got a call from the District Superintendent over the churches in our district. He and his wife wanted to take us out to lunch. The district office was a couple of hours from us, so it was arranged we would meet them half way at a restaurant. We were excited, because we would get to meet them on a one-to-one basis to get to know them a little better. Lunch was served, and after we started eating the District Superintendent said the reason for this meeting was that the Lord had spoken to him. The Lord had spoken to the existing Missionary President of that District to step down. It was coming up time for an election to replace her. She had held this position for many years. The Lord had spoken to the Superintendent that I was to take her place.

Well, he had to be kidding. I couldn't take this position. You see I was not qualified in any way. I was a fairly new sold-out child of God, new to the denomination, and I knew nothing about the different ministries that it took to keep the district operating. Not to mention, I was a new pastor's wife. I remember telling the District Superintendent, "You have to be kidding me! I know nothing about any of this, and you are asking me to run for District Missionary President?" In my panic, forgetting for a moment my commitment to God, my eyes were on myself. My husband, who was no help said, "Sure, she can do it." I sat there stunned and thought they had all lost their mind. I felt like Moses in the Bible as he told the Lord he could not speak in front of people. I did not know how to run a Missionary Convention, and my mind went whirling with I cant's.

The District Superintendent kept talking to me. He got me to agree to at least go to the next council meeting that was coming up soon. All I had to do was go there and meet the people in the council and listen. It ended up the presiding president was not able to be there. I agreed to go, but only to listen to make them happy.

I went to the meeting, and they were all very nice to me. The table was full of people. I did not know one of them. That scared me; I might have to say something. I was listening to everything being discussed at the meeting, but also talking all through the meeting to the Lord in my mind, "Lord this is way over my head; I can't do this." Then they finished their meeting and turned to talk to me. The council members started questioning me wanting me to tell them about myself. I told them a little about myself and that I was new at this walk with the Lord, and I certainly did not know anything about this part of the Missionary Society. I had become familiar with the missionary ministry at the church level. I let them know I did not have a clue what to do if I agreed to take this position, and if I got voted in. Some of them started crying. They looked at each other and said, "She is perfect for the position." The District Superintendent and this table full of people had lost their minds. I went home, and the Lord started speaking to me to trust Him. I was scared, but I agreed to let them put my name up to be voted on. No one knew me on the Northern Michigan District; someone else would get the position. I had nothing to worry about.

My walk with the Lord was about to get even deeper. I was voted in by almost a 100%. The District Missionary society was struggling financially when I was voted in as President. When I met with the exiting president to get the files of paperwork and the procedures on how to be a District Missionary President, she told me at convention time I would have to pound the floor to get enough money to meet budgets for the year. I told her I was not going to pound any floor for anything. The Lord got me into this, and if He wanted the money to come, He was God; He would bring it. I went home with a car full of boxes of papers. I hate wading through paperwork. So here we are Lord, what are You going to do now?

Soon after the convention, the council meet to start the New Year. The Lord led me to a devotional to start out the meeting with, and I was to leave the rest to Him. I had found the paper telling me how to open and close a meeting. I made a copy of the paper and took it so I could read it and get it right. Little did I know, I was soon to find out why the Lord had put me in that position. I was learning to listen carefully to the Lord. I needed Him more than ever. I told the council that day that not only were they going to have to do their own jobs, but help me do mine also. It was then that I was told the previous

President had been in her position for so long she was doing everyone's job. She would often change what the others did do. No one felt needed and the spirit had left. That was why I was perfect for the job. I knew nothing, and the council could come together and pull together as a fully- functioning body again. Each one would take ownership of his part. God is so good, but He sure can scare me to death at times.

Sharon, who was the District Missionary secretary, took me under her wing. She was like an angel sent from God to mentor me. I began learning.

Meantime back at the church, there was an elderly couple in the church who were both retired pastors in the denomination. I had met the wife at the council meeting. Dorothy was the treasurer for the District Missionary Council. We became close to Dorothy and Dominic; they had one son who lived hours away from them in the South. They were in their eighties. The Lord laid it upon our hearts to help them out when they needed it, and as they drove about thirty miles to our church, we would have them in for dinner after church on Sunday.

It was only a few months after we had become good friends with this couple that Dorothy started not feeling well. She ended up in the hospital. Her husband Dominick was beginning to lose his eyesight. When we learned she was in the hospital, we went and got Dominick to come stay with us until Dorothy could be released. Dorothy kept getting worse. Dorothy had to be transferred to the Ann Arbor Hospital in the lower part of Michigan about three hours away. We still had Dominick living with us, so on Monday's, Wednesday's and Fridays I would drive him to see Dorothy.

Dorothy had gotten mad at us for taking in Dominick; she wanted him to stay at their little farm way out in the country by himself. He was not able to take care of himself for any length of time. We had noticed some memory issues with Dominick and he could not see to drive. When I took Dominick, to the hospital, I would take Dominic to Dorothy's room, say "Hi," and find a nurse to see how Dorothy was doing. The hospital soon realized that there was no one to talk to about all that was going on and a social worker came to talk to me. Since I was caring for Dominic, I became the one the hospital employees talked to about Dorothy's condition. After making sure Dominic had all he needed, I would leave Dominic and Dorothy alone to visit. I would take my Bible and head for the hospital cafeteria. I would find a table far off in a corner in the cafeteria where I would not be in anyone's way.

I was sitting there working on a Bible Study to present to the ladies of the church, when I felt someone walk up and stand right beside me. I looked up to see a well-dressed lady standing there pulling a briefcase behind her. We said "Hi" to each other. She said, "The Lord has directed me over here to talk with you, may I sit down?" I scooped up my books and papers in a pile to make room for her. She said, "I have some questions I have been asking The Lord about, and I am not getting any answers. You may be able to help me." Since I had been the owner-operator of a beauty shop for twenty years, I had learned how to be a good listener. She started talking, and I listened. I did not have an answer and did not feel the Lord give me an answer. I told her I would help her pray that the Lord would bring her the answer she needed. We prayed, and she left.

This lady was a pharmaceutical salesperson and lived in another state. That hospital was on her circuit. I did not get her name or really not much information about her, I never really expected to ever see her again. I went home and kept lifting her up and her situation in prayer. I was still in the habit of rising at 4:00 a.m. and going to the church altar to pray. While in my studies a couple days later, the Lord brought the answer the lady at the hospital needed. I did not have a clue how to get the answer to her. I was praying the Lord would give her the answer. I figured my part was to pray, and I was doing that. I turned it over to the Lord, and told Him, that He brought us together the first time, and if He wanted me to give her the answer, He could bring us together again. As soon as I got Dominic to Dorothy's room on our next hospital visit, I headed to the nearest restroom and went into a stall. When I was coming out of the stall, there was the pharmaceutical salesperson walking into the restroom. She remembered me. In that huge hospital, that was always so busy, it just so happened there we were, and I told her what the Lord had directed me to tell her. She threw her arms around me; it was what she needed. We parted, and I never saw her again.

I learned a couple of lessons from this experience. First, if Dorothy had not been mad at me, I would not have been in the cafeteria; I would have been up in the room, and I would not have met that young lady. God taught me not to be upset with the instruments God may be using in our lives to work something out for His purpose. Second, the Lord has taught me this lesson time and time again over the years; it does not matter where two people live, if He wants to bring them together for His purpose, it will happen.

Dorothy ended up having to have a leg amputated. Shortly after the incident with the lady in the cafeteria, Dorothy changed and was not mad at me anymore. I became advocate over both of them for their medical purposes. Dorothy was finally well enough to be moved to a nursing home back in our home town, West Branch, Michigan. I was having to drive her back and forth to Ann Arbor, Michigan for her checkups, and they were fitting her with an artificial leg. We got a call late one night from the nursing home, Dorothy had taken a turn for the worse. They had transported her back to Ann Arbor to the hospital. We got Dominic up and we took off for the hospital.

When we got to the hospital, the doctors did not know what was going on with Dorothy. Toward morning, when I went in to see Dorothy, she was out of her coma; she motioned for me to come over and lean over so she could talk to me. She was really weak and could hardly speak above a whisper. I went over to her and bent down to listen. She said, "Jesus came and told me He is going to take me home with Him today." She was so happy. It was not long after we had to leave her because we could only be there with Dorothy a few minutes each hour. We had to take turns going in with her also. It was about thirty minutes after I had left her when we were informed, she had passed. The Lord had spoken again, and did what He said He was going to do.

Dominic wanted to stay with us and begged us to keep him. So, I agreed that as long as I could handle him, I would. He had me put as power of attorney over him, and this meant I had to handle the selling of their little farm and had to deal with having an auction sale to dispose of all their material goods. Dorothy and Dominic had planned on one day opening a little antique store. So, their upstairs and a little barn out behind the house were full of antiques they had collected for years. The neighbors that lived next to Dorothy and Dominic were wonderful help, and we became good friends. I put the farm up for sale with a realtor after we had gotten it all cleaned out.

A few days later after, I had put the farm in a realtor's hands, early in the morning a call came in, and my husband answered the phone. It was a man, and he wanted to talk to me. I got on the phone, and he proceeded to tell me that he was going to buy Dorothy and Dominic's farm. I told him that was great and gave him the realtor's name. He said, "No, you don't understand. I am going to buy the farm. I am not going through a realtor." He told me he talked to Dorothy, and he told her he was buying the farm when they were gone. Again, I told him the realtor's name and told him to go buy it. That's when he proceeded to tell me that if I did not do what he wanted me to, he was going to take my life. My husband was standing there and heard this man yelling at me on the phone, He took the phone from me and hung it up. I was a little shaken. A few hours later, the neighbor who lived next to Dorothy and Dominic's farm called to tell us that this man was a drug dealer in the area. He had told some neighbors what he was going to do. He had them all afraid of him. He had probably told Dorothy what he was going to do, and she agreed because she was afraid of him too. It crossed my mind that he had told Dorothy what he was going to pay for the farm. The price the realtor had put on it was not what he planned on paying.

The next day was Sunday morning, and we were getting ready for church when the phone rang. I answered it. It was the neighbor lady from out by Dorothy and Dominic's farm with whom I had made friends. When I answered she shouted, "God has protected you. You will be alright. He is dead." I could not believe what I was hearing. This guy who had threatened me, was forty-two years old with no health problems that anyone knew of. He just had a massive coronary standing in front of the mirror shaving that morning. She kept thanking the Lord for His protection. This guy threatened to take my life and was telling the people around the neighborhood about it, and the next morning he was the one dead. When I got over hearing the news, I dropped into a chair and had to praise the Lord for what He had done. It came to mind, "Just trust me, I have you."

The Lord was teaching me to trust Him no matter how difficult the situation may be. He was there, and He is in control. The more I read my Bible, the more the Lord was showing me how He really is in control. The sovereignty of God was not anything I had heard being preached or taught. I was reading the words "sovereign Lord" in my Bible, and they were becoming more than words written on a page to me. My husband did not believe the way I was being taught to believe, in God being sovereign. There were already problems starting in the marriage, and the way I was believing was making the wall higher between us. I began to realize it was not me that he wanted, but what I had. I really prayed for our marriage believing God would change me or him. I knew God had put us together. I was beginning to learn that God's ways of doing and thinking are not what we would expect He would do. I was enrolled in the Lord's school, learning from the experiences He engineered for me to go through.

The first study Bible I bought to read was a NIV Study Bible. I remember standing in the Christian bookstore looking at all those Bibles. I stood there and asked the Lord, "What do You want me to read first?" Almost everyone I knew would not pick up anything but the Kings James version to read. I was to learn that the word "sovereign" is not in the Kings James version. The NIV has "sovereign God" all through it. Because I was reading the NIV, I was constantly reading "sovereign God." God was teaching me as I had asked Him to do, and He was letting me live through circumstances that would drive the lessons even deeper. I never dreamed I was going to go through such rejection. It was His grace and strength that I held my ground, standing for the truths I was learning. I would never have thought that the scripture would bring division between my husband and me. *(Matthew 10: 34-36, Don't assume that I came to bring peace on the earth. I did not come to bring peace, but a sword. For I came to turn a man against his father, a daughter against her mother, a daughter-in-law against her mother-in-law; and a man's enemies will be the members of his household. CSB).* It was going to be awhile before I would read this scripture. When I did get to it, this scripture jumped off the page at me.

I was a long way from perfect, but I loved this man with all my heart. I was determined to try to be the best wife possible. I knew the Lord had brought this person in my life; I was going to love him with all I had in me. I had learned from losing Bob how quickly life can be snatched away from us. I had not learned to put the Lord first in my life, where He wanted to be. I, without knowing what I was doing as of yet, was trying to put my husband on the pedestal meant for God only, and God was not going to let my husband up there with Him.

My husband believes that we live in a fallen world, and I know we do, but he believes things in our lives happen by chance. This was not what I was learning in my Bible. I love Isaiah 45. The last part of verse 6 reads (*"I am the Lord, and there is no other. 7, I form light and create darkness, I make success and create disaster, I am the Lord, who does all these things. CSB).* I was learning to believe the Bible and what it said literally. I take His word as truth. I got a grip that God put His son on a cross for us and was willing for His Son to take the punishment for our sins that Jesus did not deserve. He opened the way for us to have a personal relationship with God through the Holy Spirit. He is willing to put us through whatever it will take to purify us. He will do what He wants whether it makes sense to us or not. His ways are not our ways, and I was learning these truths through real life circumstances.

6

DOES PRAYER WORK?

Reading a book one day these words jumped out at me, "Lord, come down out of heaven and do what only You, Lord, can do." By this time, I was spending more and more time praying. I was spending an hour or more in the mornings and at night in prayer. Our house connected to the church, and I would take my Bible, go over to the altar, turn on the pulpit light and pray at the altar. I felt close to my Lord there, and it was quiet. There was no TV playing and nothing to distract me, just the Lord and me. I had asked the Lord during my prayer time if prayer was real? I remembered asking the Lord if prayer was real when I asked Him to come out of heaven and do what only He could do. *I was learning to pay attention to what questions were coming into my mind from God, and then watching how God was going to answer the questions. I have come to believe when God wants me to pay particular attention to something, and He wants to show me about Himself, He inspires me to ask a question. Then when*

He brings the answer, there is no doubt it was He answering the questions in His way. He lets me see Him working in the way only He can. He gets the credit and praise for what He has done, and I am learning who He is. He was teaching me there are no coincidences. He is sovereign over and in all things in the heavens and on the earth. On a Monday during devotion time, I felt instructed to write down and start praying, "Lord come down out of heaven and do what only You, Lord, can do." So, I wrote this in large letters on a sheet of paper and propped it up on a cabinet where I could see it often to remind me to pray. I thought, "The Lord is wanting me to pray this because He is really going to do something in the church or open my husband to see what He was teaching me." I was excited to see what He was going to do.

That Saturday we had to make a hospital call to see one of our ladies from the church who was in one of the big hospitals in the Southern part of Michigan three hours away. My husband had been with another person most of the night who had been taken to another hospital in a little town near where we lived. He was tired, so I drove on this day so he could sleep some. We had been driving about an hour in our little Ford Aspire. I was driving the speed limit of seventy miles an hour on the expressway. It was a Saturday morning, and there was a bit of traffic on the highway. We were approaching Bay City, Michigan, and the expressway had turned into three lanes. We were coming up to an off and on ramp. I noticed a ton dually pickup truck coming on the highway, so I got over in the far-left lane which gave the driver of the dually two lanes to enter on. The next thing I knew, I looked to my right to see this truck almost on top of me. I remember going over more to the left which put me off the road on the edge. My husband woke up at that moment to see this trucks mirror about to hit our car. I looked in front of me, and all I could see was the guard rail and the cement wall of the overpass. We were headed right for it. We had our little dog with us and Dominic sleeping in the back seat of the car. All of a sudden, our car had made a forty-five degree turn to the right and was heading back across the three lanes. The next instant we somehow flipped around, and we were heading back to the left side of the highway. It was like we were picked up and turned around, so we were heading back in the direction we just came from. This time we were under the overpass sitting cross ways of the road. The truck that had almost hit us was nowhere to be seen. All I remember was hearing the Lord tell me to hit the brakes. I did, and we stopped under the overpass looking at a cement wall in front of us.

All I remember is from the time I saw the side of the truck inches from our car, until I was told to hit the brakes, I did nothing. There was a peace that was unreal in that little car. We did not get jerked around. Dominic, the retired minister who was living with us, was dozing in the back seat with our little Bichon lying beside him. Neither of them, woke up until my husband jumped out of the car in the middle of the expressway. The car was sitting crossways the three lanes when I looked to my left. I was looking back down the highway we had just traveled over, and I saw several cars heading for us. I screamed at my husband to get back in the car. I had to get out of the way. He jumped back in. We could smell hot rubber like I have never smelled before. There did not seem to be any flat tires, so I drove to the next gas station. We pulled off the highway to look the car over. The tires were perfectly fine. We were sure there would be some evidence showing on the tread of the tires, to indicate all we had been through. We could not find a thing wrong anywhere. We drove on the last hour and a half to the hospital, and when we got out in the parking lot, there was still a strong smell of hot rubber, so we checked everything again. Everything was perfectly fine.

It was really late when we got home that night. I did not get over to the church to pray. The next morning. I was at the altar at 4:00 a.m., my usual time to meet my lord. I was giving thanks and praising the Lord for the miracle we witnessed the day before. I heard the Lord speak to me, "You wanted to know if prayer was real; you were praying for your own life." My prayer, "Come down out of heaven and do, what only You, Lord, can do." It is exactly what He did. Is prayer real? Oh Yes! I was learning He still works in supernatural ways. He will let us see Him working when we are earnestly seeking Him with all of our hearts. There is nothing impossible for my Lord. He is completely sovereign and still works in supernatural ways.

My husband was not ordained yet. The time had come for a review to be taken for him to be ordained. My husband was not too happy; the District Superintendent told him he felt the Lord wanted him to wait another year before he could be ordained. My husband had taken classes offered by the Nazarene District, so he could be ordained, but my husband wanted to get a college degree.

This was going to mean going to classes and studying besides what he needed to do for the church. He was going to be taking a full load each semester for a four-year degree. I was beginning to get insight into why the Lord was not allowing me to go to work. I would be visiting people in our church in the hospital and going to be with them during surgeries or any major procedures. I had been making hospital calls with my husband, so it was not going to be much different for me. Traveling with my husband on these calls helped me get familiar with the different hospitals. I was comfortable with having to drive long distances by myself. By this time, I knew where I was going.

I had worked for years and wanted to go back to work. When I fell and broke my wrist, I had read in my Bible, not to make a commitment to the Lord and break it. I had given myself to the Lord to do with as He chose to do, and I knew He did not want me working outside of what He was having me do in the church. It seemed temptation to get a job was around every corner. I had worked at a bank for five years up until I had my first baby. Every time I walked into the bank there was a sign for help wanted, and stores everywhere with signs wanting help. I had worked my way through high school at a variety store. I have always liked working. The broken wrist was still fresh in my mind to remind me that if He wanted me to have a paying job, He would make sure I knew I could take the job. I was not to go seeking one. I used every spare minute reading my Bible or any other books He put in my hands to help me grow spiritually. After about a year at our first church, He finally opened a little work for me here and there.

The person who did hair at the local funeral home had to quit. They were having trouble getting someone who would do hair on deceased people. I had apprenticed with the lady going to the funeral home to do hair with her, and I had done the hair for all my customers who passed while I was their hair dresser. I had learned what to do, and this did not bother me. If I did not know the deceased person, I always wondered where their soul had gone. I worked for this funeral home until we moved away. Another part-time job I was allowed to have, was with a lady in our church who catered weddings and parties. She had family that helped her, but if there was going to be a job for over two hundred fifty people, I would go and help. All the food was made from scratch. I love cooking, so I enjoyed helping her and working with her family.

Dominic had been put into the hospital with dizzy spells, and I was going to his room to see him. He was in the West Branch Hospital in the town where we lived. As I was walking down the hall to Dominic's room, I passed a room and caught sight of a woman I had seen in the church a few times. She was sitting there with her husband. I stopped in to talk to them. We had been praying for him; we had heard that he had been in the hospital in Tawas, Michigan where they were visiting, because they thought he was having a heart attack. When he was put in the Tawas hospital, they had to draw blood to see what was going on. The lab technician tried several times. A doctor was finally called in to try. The man was poked twenty-one times before they could get blood from him. They tried his head, hands, arms, and feet, everywhere. The doctors could find nothing wrong with the man and finally sent him home. He had another episode with symptoms of a heart attack after he got back home in West Branch and he had just been admitted and put in a room in the West Branch, hospital where I was on my way to see Dominic. While I was talking to this man and his wife, a lab technician came wheeling a cart to draw blood. The patient said, "Oh no, not this again." No one told me to leave, so I stood there to watch. The technician started toward the man's bed to put the tourniquet on his arm and I heard, "Pray I put the needle in." I stepped back behind the curtain and prayed that the Lord would direct the needle in. The next thing I heard was the man shouting, "It went in the first time, and there is blood." I stepped back around the curtain, and his wife looked at me and said, "You stepped back and prayed, didn't you?" I said, "Yes, I did. I felt the Lord direct me to pray for Him to direct the needle in." We got to see the Lord work a miracle that day. The doctors determined he had a heart problem. The person was held a couple of days and released with medication. I was learning that God works through prayer. He will direct what to pray; we need the ears to hear.

These people were not real regular church attenders, but they were there the next Sunday and the guy could not wait to testify what the Lord had done for him. They began taking their walk with the Lord seriously, and their church attendance, along with testimony, was evidence of it.

I kind of expected there to be some complaints about the pastor not showing up when people were sick or in the hospital, but that never happened. No one ever fussed about the preacher's wife showing up at the hospital instead of the preacher. I think they figured out that maybe the Lord would listen to the preacher's wife's prayers, as well as, the preachers. I was beginning to learn the more time a person spends with the Lord in prayer, the more the Lord will let a person see Him work in a supernatural way. I was forming this pattern of spending as much alone with Him as I could get each day, that has remained to this day. How much does a person want to see Jesus? How close we walk with our Lord will show in our daily lives. Anything that takes away from our time with the Lord becomes an idol. I had read in a book about how people like John Wesley and George Whitfield spent hours in prayer, and how they were used to bring on great revivals. I was praying for family members and people all around me to be brought into a real personal relationship with the Lord. I was learning that my attitudes that were not pleasing to the Lord would have to be purified, so that His Holy Spirit would be free to pray through me for these people. I could slowly see my passions changing. I could see myself desiring more time with the Lord.

As District Missionary President I was putting out newsletters once a month to all the churches in our District. My favorite part of the newsletter was finding a devotional to insert that might help people to grow in their walk with the Lord. I was able to talk to missionaries all over the world. Once a year we would bring a missionary to the Northern Michigan District for deputation. If they did not have transportation, I would travel with them taking them from church to church each night in a different section of the Northern Michigan District. Our District covered from the middle of Michigan all the way up, and including, the Upper Peninsula of the state. The Nazarene churches in each area would come together, and we would have a service. There would be a freewill offering to help support the missionaries when they went back on the field. I had asked the churches ahead of time, if a few people would meet before each service to pray for the service and the missionary. Some were happy to, but others said there was not time. I began to notice something. In the places where there was prayer before the service, the missionary's message would be totally different from where there was no prayer. He would be more on fire where there was prayer. Now the three of us would always pray, but I was learning, the more people praying, the more the Lord would move. I had made friends with an elderly lady who would travel with me if the male missionary did not have his wife with him. We witnessed that when the church as a whole would take the time to come a little earlier to pray at the altar; those people received a whole different message.

About the end of the week of traveling, I asked the missionary why in some churches he gave only facts and statistics about the work. When some in the congregation would come early and pray with us, he would share more of what was going on in their daily lives on the mission field. His answer to me was, "I have prepared a format that I follow to present to all the churches I visit. Most of what I write are the statistics about how many were reached for Christ, and what was accomplished in the last year concerning facts and figures in the churches, schools, and hospitals that our ministry was a part of." When there was corporate prayer, I feel the Holy Spirit direct me to speak about the personal encounters our family had while ministering to the people." Sometimes they had to deal with witchcraft from the local villages. It could keep us on the edge of the seat. Of course, the missionaries told lots of stories of what happened in their ministries as we were in the car traveling to the different churches each day. It made the traveling time pass quickly, for his stories were endless. He answered my question, "When we pray the Lord changes my presentations." Again, it came to me, we get as much as we are willing to invest. How much do we want? How much of God do we want in our churches, in our personal lives? Do we give Him the time He so deserves? I was learning that when we give more of ourselves to Him, He gives more of Himself to us.

The Lord was teaching me the power of prayer and the responsibility we have as His children to pray. God does not work unless we pray. So, if a pastor does not have much of the Holy Spirits fire in him when he or she is preaching, whose fault is it? If the pastor is not a praying pastor, more than likely the church ends up not being a praying church. People want to complain about the pastor, but, if they ever bring the matter before the Lord, the finger may point back at them. Have they prayed for their pastor? There is a scripture in the Bible that tells us what to do. (*2 Chronicles 7: 14, and my people who are called by My name, humble themselves, pray and seek my face, and turn from their evil ways, then I will hear from heaven, forgive their sin, and heal their land. CSB).* What if the Lord really means what He says? What makes Him move on His people's behalf? It takes our obedience to what He demands in His word.

We must humble ourselves. What does that really mean? I learned to allow the Holly Spirit daily to search deep within my being for anything in me that is not pleasing in His sight and to clean it out. God knows our motives even when we don't want to acknowledge them. He will only answer our prayers if it will bring Him the glory. I learned to think of these sins like a cancer that I wanted cut out before it could grow and take my life. I had seen how cancer eats away a person's body when I watched the brain tumor destroy my husband's body. We can pray, but I learned that first, the praying vessel has to be clean. I was learning that it was not my prayers God wanted or would answer, but the prayers of His Son, prayed through me by the Holy Spirit. I needed to die out to self, allow the Holy Spirit to pray through me, and answers would come. God had opened my heart to seek Him and He was engineering the circumstances in my life. I was not only reading about what He expects from His children, again I have to repeat, it seemed I was getting to live out those scriptures in my life.

There were many hard trials that seemed to come from every direction. I had read in Oswald Chambers devotional to expect lots of bumps and bruises as we are being hammered into a more Christ-like character. God would use the common-place people and circum-stances to work out His purpose in our lives. I had a lot of growing to do; in time I learned it was through prayers of different people for one reason or another that kept me pressing forward, no matter what kept coming. Each trial that came was pushing me closer into the Lord and making me desire Him more. The Lord revealed to me one morning as I was praying at the altar, that it was the prayers of those dear people in my beauty shop praying for me when my husband was dying, that started His work of drawing me closer to Him. I had a few people who walked with the Lord and were no stranger to a life of prayer. If my family ever prayed, they were not in any shape for the Lord to answer their prayers. I know I was the first born-again believer on my father's side. Having the beauty salon put me in the hearts and paths of people who could truly pray, and God would hear their payers and answer.

Now I was District Missionary President over thrity-four churches. As I traveled with the missionary, I had many people who had a real heart for missions come up and tell me they were praying for me. They understood that missions were the heartbeat of our Lord. They could feel the heartbeat of the Northern Michigan District was not where it should be. I have talked about God engineering our circumstances to please Him. He revealed to me that when He wanted me to get serious with Him, the trials got harder, but He also brought the people to pray for me. This gave me the desire to cling to Him even more. Now He had moved me from the beauty shop to this new position quickly, which put me in the path of even more praying people. He was going to move me even deeper with Him. I was learning more truths about The Lord, as well as, what I looked like in His eyes. How could God love a person like me? God, all knowing, was engineering the circumstance, pointing out these things in my life that were.3 not pleasing to Him. The prayers of these people, though they may not have realized, were giving me the strength and desire to run towards the Lord, not away from Him. Some of the people in the church who, could see some of the trials I was under, were praying also. God had me where He wanted me, and I could see the plans I had for my life fading in the dust faster each day.

7

FEAR

Not long after traveling with my lady friend and the missionary, I received a letter informing me that there was going to be three days of training for all the new District Missionary Presidents from all over the United States and other countries. This training would be held in Kansas City, Missouri. I was going to have to fly to district headquarters alone. We were living in West Branch, Michigan. I had flown quite a bit with groups going on tours and with family. I would have to fly alone on this trip. At first, I said, "No, I am not going alone!" My husband said, "Yes you are. You will be fine." I had made the trip with the missionary traveling around unfamiliar areas fine, because the lady traveling with us knew her way around the state to the different churches. No one could go with me on this trip.

All the things that could happen started flooding my mind. I was flying where someone from headquarters was supposed to pick me up. Who would that be, and how would I know them? The Nazarene Headquarters had made all the flight arrangements for me. I had never made my own arrangements to fly; someone else always was in charge of that. Even though my head said, "No, I can't do this," I could feel the Lord telling me He would be with me. I just needed to trust Him.

All my information and ticket came through to me. As I had said, daily, I was under trials. I was realizing that my husband did not marry me because he loved me. He had other motives and the Lord brought him into my life knowing that. All that was going to happen was going to drive me closer to Himself and teach me how sovereign He really is. When it was time for me to leave, I had to drive myself four hours to my mom's house, and she would take me to the Detroit, Michigan airport, I would fly out from. I asked my husband if he wanted my flight number and information of when and where I was going to be. His answer was, "No, what do I want that information for. You will be fine." When the time came, I loaded up and left. I prayed all the way to my mom's house as she lived not too far from the airport and I could leave my car with her. I was going to have to find my way around the Detroit Metro Airport by myself to get to my plane. I was praying, "You have gotten me into this Lord. You have to take care of me." My mom did take all the information about my flight, which made me feel a little better. Someone knew where I was, besides the Lord.

I usually love to fly; this day was different. My mind was going ninety miles an hour between praying and questioning, "When I get there, where will I go? Do I get my luggage first? What do I do? How big is the airport?"

Headquarters did not know who would come to get me. I was just told someone would be there, that was all. I remember the panic and what I was thinking, but hardly remember the flight itself. Finally, we landed at the airport in Kansas City. I was praising the Lord, as well, because I did not have to switch planes along the way.

As I was coming out of the plane to head toward the luggage area there was a person standing with a big sign with the words "Nazarene Headquarters" written on it. I ran toward him and told him my name. The person holding the sign said to me when he learned my name, "Finally we have found you!" I said, "What do you mean, you have finally found me?" The young man said, "We have had someone at the airport every time there was a plane coming from your direction looking for you all day." He helped me get my luggage, and we headed for Headquarters. When the young man took me into the main office to let them know I was there, they all came over to me, and I got the biggest welcome. I said to them, "You mean I was lost?" They proceeded to tell me what had happened.

Headquarters was having to get all the new District Missionary Presidents who were coming in from all over the United States, Canada, etc. Somehow all my flight information had gotten misplaced. They knew I was coming and the direction I was coming from, just not my flight information. Someone had called my husband to see if he could help them. He had no information to give them.

When I was taken to my room where I would be staying for a few days, I began getting over the shock of finding out I really had been lost. I began praising the

Lord that He really did have everything under His control. It came across my mind, "See I always know where you are. I will take care of you. Trust Me!" My Lord is sovereign and in control. Learning it one way does not mean that there will not be a dozen or more other ways we are going to be put to the test for Him to show us how faithful He is. The flight back to Detroit was a much more enjoyable flight.

Another fear was soon to rear its ugly head and scare me to death. The time was fast approaching for a District meeting where I was supposed to speak in front of a group. I was so scared of speaking in front of large groups of people. Thinking that, I was soon going to have to get up and speak in front of all those people, wet my nerves on edge. I started to break out in hives from my head to my feet. I was a mess. I ended up in the emergency room with the doctor trying to find a place to give me a shot of steroids. The hives were huge, and the doctor finally guessed where the vein might be. Thank the Lord the doctor hit it. I was sure praying for the Lord's help. I had to spend a couple of hours there. The steroids helped me enough so that my face looked like me the next morning when it was time to go. All I can say, is the Lord helped me make it through the meeting. I do not remember much about it.

The next time I had to speak was at District Convention where all the churches came together. I had to lead the Missionary Convention, sitting up on stage in front of the whole assembly and direct the meeting. The night before we were to leave, I found myself on another trip back to the emergency room. This time I had hives ninety percent of my body, inside and out, from head to foot, giant hives. My breathing was being blocked because of the internal hives in my sinuses. I never knew that hives could affect a person internally. I had to have oxygen until they could get the hives to go down in my sinuses so I could breathe. As I was lying on the little table in the emergency room waiting for the steroids to take effect, Job from the Bible story came to mind. I had read a book about Job a few weeks before this night. The part of Job having all those sores all over his body flashed through my mind. He had to take a broken pot to scrap his sores. I was thanking the Lord that, at least I had medication and doctors to help me through my situation. I was advised to go see my doctor for continued help. This could be an ongoing issue with me.

The District Superintendent would call to make sure I was going to make it to the meetings. I told him I would be there one way or another. The Lord always had me on my feet and going every time I had to speak at a meeting. I did not know He was teaching me a lesson, and I was learning this lesson the hard way.

At the first District Assembly that I presided over, the treasurer announced that we had meet the goal for that year's budget. I did not have to pound the floor for the money needed to fulfill our Districts obligation to the General Churches Mission Fund, like I was told by the last president I would have to do. Praise the Lord, God did it.

The whole assembly lasted two days. by the time each Ministry of the Church had their time to report. The first time I was over the missionary portion of the Assembly we were given two hours for our segment. I don't think I could have taken any longer. The Lord kept me alive and raised the money we needed. I was praising Him all weekend.

The Lord was teaching me that He didn't need me to bring the money, He needed me to be obedient and pray. I had to be a willing vessel, but He would work the miracles.

Returning home after the District Assembly I went to see my doctor, and he gave me a steroid packet to have on hand. This went on for about a year with the hives before I had to speak. When I went back to my doctor after he had been treating me for the hives several times, he told me, "Vicki, you are going to have to get out of this position, or give it to the Lord. If you don't, this will kill you." The doctor was serious, and I knew it. I could not keep taking steroids, and I knew without a doubt that the Lord had called me to take this position. I was alone in the car, and I was talking to the Lord out loud. "Lord, if you really want me to be speaking in front of people, Father God. You are going to have to take this fear away from me, or I am going to be seeing You real soon." I knew I could not quit unless He released me. He was not releasing me, and I kept praying, and telling Him He had to give me peace when I had to speak in front of groups of people.

A few weeks later I had to speak again at a District workshop. I noticed the night before I had no hives. When it was my turn to get up and speak, it was all different. I had a peace over me like I had never felt before. I was still speaking, but in my head, I was praising the Lord, for I knew He was the one who had made the change. I heard the Lord speak softly through my head, "All you had to do was ask Me." *(James 4: 2b. You do not have because you do not ask. CSB).* There was another change I had never felt before, He was anointing me, and I was adding things I had never thought of saying until they came out of my mouth. I had been staying right with what I had written down on note cards until this time. I could feel a peace, and, much to my amazement, I enjoyed it. Now this was really a God movement. I could look right at the people and not over their heads or off somewhere. God was talking right to the people through me. I could feel it. I was learning to ask for what I need from Him in detail. If we know it is His will, ask and He will answer.

The Lord will show Himself to us in so many ways if we truly seek Him. Another time was about to come, I was going to see the Lord work in a way that only He could do. One evening we were sitting at home when the phone rang, and I answered it. It was Paul, an elderly man who came to our church. His son, who was away at college, came to church with Paul when he came home for visits. Paul was telling my husband that his son was drinking, and maybe on drugs also. Paul was afraid that his son would harm him in some way, and he wanted us to talk to his son, Rick. We prayed, called the church secretary to tell her what we knew about the situation, and we went out to Paul's. At least someone had an idea where we were.

I will tell you here, I am about 4 feet 10 inches tall and weigh about 120 lbs. We went into Paul's house. Rick, Paul's son, met us at the door. Rick was a college football player, and a really big guy. He was high on something with a bottle of beer in his hand. My husband said to me, "You stay in the kitchen with Rick, and I will go see about Paul." I invited Rick to sit at the kitchen table with me, and he did. I sat across from him. I asked him what was going on. He mumbled something. I kept talking to him and said, "Rick you have been in church most of your life; you know this is not pleasing to the Lord." He was just staring at me and would try to mumble something. He had set the beer bottle down on the table but still had a grip on the beer bottle. All of a sudden he blurted out, "What is wrong with me? I want to hit you with this beer bottle. I can't get it off the table. I want to swear at you and I can't even do that." I remember telling Rick, "Well, Rick you know what is the matter. The Lord will not allow you to hurt me." He jumped up, had to leave his beer bottle on the table because he still was not able to pick it up, and ran out of the house; then drove off somewhere.

Because I had been reading my Bible about the Lord working supernaturally and listening to the missionaries' stories and reading our missionaries' books telling how they saw God work in such miraculous ways, I sat amazed for a while at the table. Because God was letting me see Him work in such absolutely amazing ways, I was learning to trust Him.

Rick would have hurt me, if he could have. He eventually did break his dad's ribs. When Paul found Rick stealing checks from his check book and tried to stop him, Rich hurt his dad. He had wanted money the night we were there, but it was not long before the demands escalated from demanding money from his father to forging his father's name on checks. He ended up in state prison for a few years. The local jail was close to where we lived: I had been cutting Paul's and Rick's hair. An officer from the jail called and asked me if I would come over and cut Rick's hair during the time he was waiting to be sentenced. I liked Rick, that night was the first and only time I had ever seen him in this state. He was always good to talk to at church and when I cut their hair. I did this until he was sentenced to state prison. I took him Christian material to read, and prayed and talked about the Lord with him. I do not know what happened to him after that. We went once to the state prison to visit him soon after he was transferred, but we soon left that church and area.

After my husband became ordained, he wanted to move from the area where we were, so he talked to the District Superintendent to see if there was another church open. He wanted a bigger church. A church was opening up soon whose pastor was leaving the ministry because of health issues. The church was located in the Upper Peninsula of Michigan, so we were assigned to that church. I never planned on moving very far away from my family, but the family always loved visiting the Upper Peninsula because it is so beautiful. Our families could come and stay with us while there. It was a little drive for them, but not too bad. We used to have to take the ferry across the Straits of Mackinaw when I was little, but with the bridge, it made it much easier to cross.

It was beautiful up there. In time I was going to have to face another fear I never anticipated. When I was little and my parents and I would go on vacations in the Upper Peninsula, my parents loved to hunt and fish. My dad loved to get miles back in the woods, and I was always so afraid we would be stranded if the car broke down, or running out of gas, running out of food. Although I loved animals, we often saw bears and heard wolves. So, getting stranded anywhere out in the middle of nowhere was a fear for me. My parents would love to haul their snowmobiles and ride for miles further north from where we lived, sometimes late into the night. By the time they got snowmobiles, I was old enough to stay home alone. I would not go with them. I'd had enough adventures with them when I was younger. I wasn't going now that I could stay home. We had a dog, and I had my horse. I would stay home and take care of them. Now, the Lord had us heading further north in the ministry.

We moved in just before Christmas. I will not forget, because there was the prettiest Christmas floral arrangement sitting on the kitchen counter when we walked in late at night. The church had a house for us to live in right next to the church. I had another surprise when we walked into the house. When we were up there to interview, we needed a new living room outfit. We decided to buy one up there, and when we got there, we were going to go get it. When I walked into the house that night, there was the new living room outfit waiting for us. It was a small town, and everyone knew everything that went on with everyone. When the people of the church found out we had bought the outfit, they had it delivered. We walked in late at night with the U-Hauls loaded with everything we owned, and we had something to sit on until the next day when we could get unloaded. My son had come to help us make this move. Dominic was still with us and we were glad to have furniture.

We lived in the North, but this was going to be twenty-two miles from Canada and was going to be a whole new way of life. If you have not lived way up North, an average snow fall at a time is about 6 feet. It gets down to -20 to -30 degrees and stays there for days and even weeks. We lived across from a school, and the parking lot would be full of snowmobiles in the winter. It was the only way the kids could get to school. We got snowmobiles to get around when the snow got really deep. It was really beautiful to go out riding after a fresh snowfall. The trees, heavy laden with snow, were breathtaking as we rode through the woods. I was beginning to enjoy snowmobile riding and adjusting to a new way of life.

I was asked to start a Women's Bible study as soon as we were unpacked, and I could find my materials. By now I loved teaching Bible studies, it made me grow, and I was able to watch others grow. I had never lived in a community that was as close as these people were. There were three other churches besides our church, in this little town. All of us would attend special events at any one of the churches. Women from other churches would attend the Bible Studies. One of the young ladies who was attending, had a baby. She hated having to miss the studies until the baby got big enough to be taken out. She had no one to leave the baby with. I agreed to go to her house once a week and present to her what we had done as a group. Her husband was not a believer. She was really seeking the Lord, and the two of us would petition the Lord together for his salvation. I sort of knew him; he would come to church occasionally with her.

The Lord had put into my hands a Bible Study series when I was at our first church, and I had taken the ladies through it there. I loved it, I started the study with these women. It was *Simply Trusting, Boldly Asking, Joyfully Following, & Quietly Resting* by Aletha Hinthorn. Being a new seeker with so much to learn myself this study really helped me grow, and I watched this study help others grow. I did not know it at the time, but the Lord was going to bring one or two ladies at each church, where we ever ministered, to me to mentor on a one-to-one basis. There is much more freedom for them to really open up, having someone to pray with them on a one-on-one basis. I was realizing that these ladies, for the first time in their lives, felt free to release burdens they were carrying. I had been listening to customers who needed someone to talk to for twenty years in my beauty shop. I had never been one to tell what was shared with me in confidence. After we moved away a few years later from the Nazarene Church in Pickford, Michigan, we got good news. A person from this church called to tell us that the husband of the young lady to whom I had taught the Bible Study, was saved. He joined the church and became the Sunday School Director. My heart leaps with joy when we get to see how God works when we are obedient.

I was in prayer one morning before church when I heard the Lord speak to me that I was to pray with three others from the church once a week. Well, who could that be? This was on a Sunday morning. I did not know everyone in the church very well yet. We had not been there very long. I told the Lord I was willing, but I did not know who to ask. He would have to bring them to me. He knew who He wanted, I didn't. Before that morning was over, three women had walked up to me and told me that they felt the Lord speak to them that they should come and ask me to meet for prayer once a week. He told me what to do, and I told Him what I wanted Him to do. I knew these ladies heard from God. I knew He called us together, and He was going to work His prayers through us. No one knew about the other. I brought all three of the ladies together and shared with them what the Lord had said to me that morning. We found out that each of us spent a good deal of time with the Lord in the mornings. We decided to have our devotions alone with the Lord, as we all usually did, and we would meet together, taking turns at each other's houses shortly after our devotion and prayer time to see what He had laid on each of our hearts to pray for.

None of us had ever done this before. All I can say is that God is awesome beyond what most of us can believe. We would write down the requests God had laid on our hearts in our personal time with Him. When we came together God had brought to each of us basically the same things to lift up to Him in prayer. *(The church grew and kept on growing after we left. They were to the point of building a bigger church when we left, which they did it.)* This church was willing to meet a little earlier on Wednesday night for prayer before Bible Study. They were willing to take time to pray. God was honored, and the people reaped the harvest.

On our day off my husband and I would sometimes go snowmobile riding to get away for a little while. The neighbor lady who lived next door to us and attended church with us would watch Dominic for me, so I could get away once in a while. My husband and I each rode our own snowmobiles. When snow was really deep, it was our source of transportation until the snowplows could get out and clean the roads. One day, on our day off, we decided to go for a ride. We had a fresh snow on the ground, and we knew it would be a great day to go.

So off we went. We decided we had not ridden out to the east end of the Peninsula. We had traveled about thirty miles or so, sometimes through woods on groomed trails, at other times on roads. The roads were not traveled or plowed, because the cabins out there were boarded up for the winter. My husband came out of the woods onto a road, and he took off at about eighty miles an hour down the road. I came out behind him, and when I got on the road, I hit the gas and rubber came flying out everywhere. I came to a halt. There was that hot rubber smell that I smelled when we almost got killed on the expressway. This time something did happen. I looked up to see the back end of my husband's snowmobile disappear over a hill. I sat there with all kinds of things going through my mind and praying, "Lord, what am I going to do?" I was there for about twenty to twenty-five minutes when I saw my husband come back over the hill. When he got up beside me, he saw the pieces of rubber belt from my snowmobile all over the place. He said, "Well, it's a good thing it was your machine that the belt broke on; yours has a spare under the hood. Mine doesn't." It took a while to get all the little chunks of rubber pulled out of all the places where they could cause trouble if left, and my husband changed the belt, and we started for home.

On the way home, I was praising the Lord when I heard again, "Trust Me, I will take care of you." Like I said before, we may learn to trust Him in one way, but be lacking in many other ways. God was reaching way back into my fears I had as a child. This time of year, the bears where hibernating, but the wolves were not, and they would be hungry. He was taking me through my fears, it seemed, one by one. I began seeing what the Lord was doing with me. It was scary, but each trial was slowly releasing me from another form of bondage, and God was setting me free.

In the first church we had, we could not find anyone to play the piano. We had to sing by prerecorded music. We had a piano player in our second church. Glenda, the lady who that played for us, was gone a lot to see family who lived elsewhere. Some of the people in the church started speaking to me to learn to play. I prayed about it and told the Lord if he wanted me to learn to play the piano, He would have to open the door and make it possible. I would do it so that we would not have to be without piano music. The church had a beautiful grand piano I could practice on. A few days after I felt lead to talk to the Lord about playing the piano, I got a call from a lady saying she heard I wanted to learn to play the piano. I told her I did. She was a retired missionary and had played the piano for years by ear. She said she would love to teach me what she knew. She would not charge me for the lessons; she did it for the Lord. I started taking lessons with her.

About a year after starting lessons with her, she told me she had gone as far with me as she knew to go. She wanted me to drive into Canada to the Conservatory where they had a wonderful music department. I prayed about it, because I would have to go to another country by myself and what if something happened? God had taken care of me this far, if this was what He wanted, He would take care of me in this situation also. I called and got in to the Conservatory and started lessons. I was driving over to Canada once a week. I was used to going over there with my husband to shop at the mall at Sault Saint Marie, Canada. I was progressing well with my piano lessons and enjoyed learning to play. I did not know, but there was a lesson coming through this too, in time.

I was still District Missionary President, because this church, we had transferred to, was in the same District. We saw how the Lord was working in our District. We were given four hours for our portion of the next year's Assembly. I had a wonderful council, and they loved doing their jobs. We saw the churches come together like never before. Those, who had plenty, helped those with little to pay the budgets. When all was added up, we had gone way over what was needed for the budgets. What an honor to see the Lord work. I never had to ask for a dime. He did not need my help, only our prayers. I was to learn later after we had moved to another church in a different district, *that the* Missionary Convention had grown to a two-day event, with all kinds of stations and activities for all ages. What wonders the Lord can do when the Body of Christ starts working in unity, and everyone uses the gifts that the Lord has given them!

8

GOD HAS HIS WAY

y husband had finished two years of college when we were at our first church. Now he had completed two more years at a college in Sault Saint Marie, Michigan, in the Upper Peninsula. He had a secular degree; He decided he wanted to go on and get a preaching degree at a Bible College. He felt the bigger the degree, the bigger the church he would be able to preach in. Reading the works of the old Holiness men, I was beginning to understand it was not about education, but personal relationship with the Lord. Spending more time in prayer, and becoming a person the Holy Spirit could intercede through, is what would make a true holiness church grow, not education. A church can grow without being Holy, but it will be as secular as the world. I was growing and was beginning to realize; my husband's goal was not to work for the sake of the Lord and God's glory but to make himself more noticed. I tried to share with him what I was learning from reading *E*

M Bounds Complete Works on Prayer. This book said that being a praying pastor was what God expected more than education. I was learning how God was working through prayer for what He had called me to do. My husband saw the results, but did not want to listen and would get mad at me. I knew he was not reading what I was reading. One day he told me, "Why don't you just let the Lord work on me?" It was time to be still.

The college he wanted to attend was in Kankakee, Ill. He called and talked to the college and took a trip to see what he had to do to go there. We had attended a couple of events there and knew the college a little. I did not want to go because it was close to Chicago. I had been to Chicago once. That was enough for me; I did not ever care to go back. Besides for him to go to college at Olivet Nazarene University, we would have to have a full-time church with a place for us to live. I thought that was not likely to happen. My mom was paying his way through college up to this point, but he could figure out how to get the money for the rest if he wanted to go badly enough. The situation between my husband and me was not good and I had made up my mind I was not going to Illinois. I would go back home closer to my family. He could go on wherever he wanted, but I was not going.

After my husband had been checking things out at the college a couple of days, he called me to let me know that there was a church thirty-two miles from the college that was open. It was in New Lenox, Ill., a suburb in the South end of Chicago. My husband had just met with the District Superintendent for that Chicago District, and he wanted us to come and interview. Oh no, this could not be. I was up the next morning earlier than usual in my praying chair. I had to talk to Jesus. He could not let this be happening. I was still taking care of Dominic, and he was requiring much more care. Now that I think about it, I think the Lord used Dominic to teach me to seek Him early in the mornings before everyone in the house got up and moving. Dominic took a lot of my time, as he was getting worse with each surgery he had to go through. I knew I was going to need a lot of extra time with the Lord that morning.

You see, I had been praying for my son's salvation. He lived down near my mom in the Detroit area. He was taking computer classes and working. He was not in a church or living for the Lord. He was so good to keep track of mom, checking in on her every day and helping her when she needed it, but he needed a personal relationship with the Lord. He was single and would come spend the weekend with us about once a month. I was sitting there fussing at the Lord, being a Moses again, and giving Him every reason, I could come up with why I should not go. The Lord spoke to me very clearly, "If you do not do what I want you to do, I do not have to answer your prayer." As soon as it was daylight, I got myself and Dominic ready and put him in the van, and off we went to go start collecting boxes so I could start packing. God had spoken; I was moving. I knew the prayer the Lord was referring to was the prayer I was praying asking the Lord to open my son's heart and save Rod. I wanted my prayer answered, and the One who would answer it spoke. My husband knew I did not want to go, so when he walked in the back entrance to the house and saw boxes stacked up, he knew the Lord must have spoken.

Dominic was getting much worse mentally. He could walk into his bedroom, shut the door behind him and could not figure out how to get back out. His sight was reduced to a pin hole out of his left eye. He had lost his right eye due to an infection. He had made the last move with us fine. His health had been declining quickly the last few months. We began to realize with the long hours of traveling in a U-Haul, this move might be too hard for Dominic to make with us. We talked with Dominic's brother in Ohio and told him our situation. His brother agreed to take him in for a month until we got settled.

We were able to get Dominic to his brothers in Ohio to stay until we were able to get moved and furniture in place and unpacked. Dominic did not want to leave us; he cried. Because I knew the Lord had spoken to me and seeing how He was opening doors, I knew we would be moving. There was no doubt in my mind now. It was as good as done. I was going to obey, because God said so, no matter what. I wanted to see my prayer answered.

We headed out for Chicago with a large U-Haul towing our truck. I was driving a small U-Haul and towing my car with our two dogs early in the morning. We got to our motel in the middle of that night, had about four hours of sleep and headed to the church parsonage to meet the people who were supposed to be there to help us unload. Here I was from one extreme to another. There was hardly any traffic in the town we moved from. Not 50 feet from the front door of the house we were moving into, was a four-lane main road leading into Chicago.

There was constant traffic night and day. There was a fire station in the next block that got more calls at night than in the day time. Houses were so close that when the neighbors used their snow blower to clean their driveway, the snow landed in ours. I was with a husband who did not want me, but I had the Lord, and I was learning, He was the only one I could count on. I had to be where He wanted me to be.

But the Lord said He does what He pleases. *(Psalms 115:3 Our God is in heaven and does whatever He pleases. Psalms 135:6 The Lord does whatever He pleases in heaven and on earth, in the seas and all the depths. CSB).* I was learning this lesson also. I was reading about the Lord leading those who were really seeking Him into the desert on a walk with Him. I never dreamed that would be me. Who am I anyway? I felt like I was worth nothing, and had been told and made to feel this way in many different ways growing up. I felt I was there for support, for the works the Lord wanted to do through my husband. After all, he was the preacher. I kept looking for the Lord to work mightily through him.

I was learning that when the Lord speaks, obey, no matter what. He does not think like we think and, we really cannot begin to know what His plans are for our lives. If we are going to be all that He has planned for us to be, we must keep walking with Him often in dark days, trusting Him every step of the way. I hate to say, He had to drag me by the hand, well, actually kick me in the backside a few times along the way. My obedience was challenged when it came to moving further away from family with a person, I was feeling a great amount of rejection from. And Chicago, "Really, Father, you want me to live in a huge city like Chicago? I am a farm girl. Remember I love the smell of barns, fields and woods. You gave me the love for animals and nature since I was born. They are shooting people driving down the expressway in Chicago." I could not believe the Lord was pressing me to move to this place. When things come upon us that shake us up, it is easy to forget Who really is in control of all things.

It did not take too long to get settled in, but we got a call from Dominic's brother. They had not seen him in a couple of years and did not realize how bad his health had gotten. They said it was too much for me to care for him anymore, and they were going to put him in a nursing home near them, so they could visit him. His niece rented a van and brought Dominic over with her to see us and to pick up his bedroom furniture and the rest of his clothes. We cried when Dominic left, but the Lord knew what was coming next, and He had cleared the way.

I had no more gotten everything unpacked and found out Dominic would no longer be living with us, when I got a call from my son Rodney in Detroit. He stopped in to check on mom that morning before work, because she was not feeling well the night before. He found her in a bad state. He called an ambulance, then me, telling me to please come quickly. He had found Mom still in bed, which was not usual for her; she was was very sick. As soon as we finished talking, I packed my suitcase, grabbed my dogs and headed out for the five-hour drive to Farmington Hills, Michigan. When I got to the hospital, the doctor came out to tell me she had a large tumor in her colon that had to come out. It turned out to be cancerous. I stayed with her a few days until I knew she was going to be okay. She was going to have to go to rehab for a week or so, and they told me they would not release her until she was able to go home and take care of herself again. Rod was there to keep track of mom. The dogs and I headed back to Chicago.

After all those years in the beauty shop listening to hurting people talk to me and tell me all their problems, they had not ever told anyone else, I wanted to help them. It seemed the ministry brought to me more hurting people who needed the Lord to help them walk through this life. People would start telling me some of what had happened in their lives when they hardly knew me, or didn't know me at all. I thought that maybe I would go to college to be a Christian counselor. I knew the only way that people can truly be healed was to get help from a Christian counselor, a person who had a relationship with the Lord. Through a Christian counselor, the Lord could minister to these hurting people. It came across my mind to see about taking classes to become a Christian counselor. I had known of a pastor who took classes and became a counselor. He was overwhelmed with people needing help. I prayed about what the Lord would have me to do. It seemed He opened the door for me to start taking classes at Olivet Nazarene University to become a Christian counselor.

9

TONGUE TIED

J started taking classes and one of the first classes I ended up taking was public speaking. Oh no, I couldn't put it off. I ended up having to take the class. I prayed, "Lord, You are going to have to get me through this." Toward the end of the semester, I learned we were each going to have to do a presentation, competing against all of the students in speech classes that semester. It was required. We had to work with pictures on a screen and all kinds of props; this was not going to be good. Having raised miniature horses, I chose to give my presentation on how the miniature horse came to be and what they were used for. The miniature horses were bred down small so they could pull the mining cars through the small tunnels underground in Europe. They were small so they could ride up and down the elevators that transported the workers. They have a much better disposition than ponies, that can be cranky. It helped that

I did not have to learn something new about my topic. I just had to get pictures and write the speech.

The night came for the final runoffs in the competition. We each had to give our speeches three times to get down to the final six students who would compete for which place we would win. I made it down to the finals with the last six students for placement. I was sitting next to a friend, and it was getting close to my turn to present my speech. Everyone was telling me how much they enjoyed the speech I had given. I said to the young lady next to me, "Between the miniature horses, me and God, we may win this." I got up and started giving my speech. Everything was going well until, all of a sudden, my mouth got so dry my tongue kept sticking to the roof of my mouth. It happened only for a few seconds, and I was fine again. But it had made me stammer for those few seconds, because I could not get my words out.

I finished my speech and was heading back to my seat. On my way back I asked the Lord, "What happened?" Immediately I got a reply from the Lord, "You put me last, I put you where you put Me," The last thing I had said to my friend before walking up to give my speech flashed before my mind. When I had spoken to her, I put the Lord last, not first. I pray I never forget this lesson. I did get the sixth-place trophy, but it broke my heart at how I had treated the Lord without thinking.

The next day students and professors were stopping me and asking me what happened. I had a testimony to share with them. Don't put the Lord last in anything. He will not be pleased, and it may cost you.

Mother healed well from her surgery. She had scheduled a cruise through the Hawaiian Islands with the group of people she always traveled with. I was able to complete one semester of classes, and I know by the grades I got the Lord was the one getting the grades through me. I loved the students and they related well with me. I was in my fifties and most of them were in their twenties. They kind of looked at me as their away-from-home mother.

Mother loved to travel and traveled all over the world with this group of people. The doctor knew mom had this trip planned. Mom took her cruise and a few days after she got home from the trip, she had an appointment to go get a check up to make sure she was still doing well. It was then that the doctor told mom he wanted her to have chemo treatments. He said all had gone well with the surgery, but the tumor was so big he wanted to make sure there were no cells that had broken off that might start another tumor. Mom was told it would be a light chemo; she should have no problems with it. She would have to go in for five straight days to get the chemo and would be able to go home each day.

My experience with Bob and chemo was not good. I had read everything I could get my hands on about chemo. I knew that it was not going to be a light dose of chemo. Mom was not a person to run to the doctor very often. I tried to talk her out of getting chemo. I wanted her to go for a second opinion somewhere else. Warnings were flaring up all over my mind. She told me she would do what the doctor said. They set her up for her first infusion the Monday after she got home from her cruise. She went and got it. Then it happened. My son went to check in on her, and mom was in bad shape in her bed. Her body was shutting down. She could barely breathe. Rod called an ambulance, and they asked her if she wanted to be put on life support. She nodded, "Yes," she did.

Rodney called me, and I headed back to Detroit again. When I got there, she was on life support and not doing well. The next day I called the college and told them what was going on. It looked like I would be with mom for a while, and I needed to drop my classes. As it turned out I was there for three months. Mom was on life support for some time but eventually was able to be taken off of it. We were encouraged when she was moved to a regular hospital room. Mom was able to talk to me and eat some. The next thing we knew, she had dropped into a coma. She was in this state a day and she passed.

When the doctor came to talk to me, I questioned the chemo he gave my mom. I told him it was not a light chemo; it was a strong one. His reply was to me, "If I would have told her what it was, she would have not let me give it to her." I was upset.

There was a lady friend of mom's who traveled with my mom. She was a lawyer. She was upset when she found out what had happened, and she tried to get the doctor's license pulled for lying to my mother. It seems in Michigan doctors can treat patients with medication or whatever and not really let a person know what they are doing, if the doctor feels it's for the best. There was nothing we could do about his lying to my mom. It cost her life.

Meantime, staying at my mother's house, I found a Nazarene church to go to while I was there. Rodney would come by and pick me up from mom's and go with me. I was there to go to church with him for the three months. God was working. He was getting established with some young people his age, and when I left Detroit to go back to Chicago, praise the Lord, Rod kept attending the church, making more friends.

After mom died it crossed my mind maybe this would be the time the Lord would let me leave my husband. The nurses had been talking to me about how short staffed they were, and it would be easy to get into nursing school. I had done a lot helping vets with our animals and helping people in our church after they got home from surgeries, changing dressings and such. I could be a nurse. Where I would take classes would be right close to where mother's house was. Mom had a small house on an acre of land in Livonia, Michigan. Rod lived close. He was alone, I had been going to church for three months at a Nazarene church not too far from where Mother's house was and made friends. I had made friends with all of mother's neighbors. We had found out the day before mom died my daughter Missy was going to have my first grandchild. I would only be two hours from her instead of five. The Lord woke me up in the middle of the night and spoke to me, "You cannot leave." I was my mother's only child, so the house was mine. It was fully furnished, so I would leave everything in Chicago for my husband. I needed nothing but my personal belongings. But the Lord said. I had to go back. My husband was talking to me only when he wanted something.

I knew I had to obey the Lord and go back to Chicago. When I got back to Chicago, my husband had a new motorcycle picked out he wanted to get. I had read several devotionals that helped me to begin to understand following the Lord is not an easy path to follow. It was going to take holding on to the Lord as tight as I could to stay obedient. As a matter of fact, I started praying He keep a tight grip on me. After all, I was learning that He is the all-powerful One. I was nothing. I was no different than the disciples who strained at the oars of their boat that stormy night when Jesus told them to cross the lake and Lazarus's sisters watching their brother die when they knew if Jesus was there, He could have saved their brother. I was being taught that when God waits, He has a reason. He is God, and He knows what His purpose is, and what He has to put us through to accomplish it. I was reading that it is the circumstances of life that He uses to mold His children to His will. The only time I could find peace was when I kept my mind stayed on the Lord, or in His word. Even while I was working, my mind was going over what I had read last. I repainted mom's house, gave furniture, dishes and clothes away to anyone who needed them and put the house up for rent through a realtor. Just in case I ever wanted or needed to live in the house again.

When I was taking classes and would be at the college library, I got to know the women who worked there. They kept wanting me to apply for a job to work at the library. There was a nighttime supervisor position opening, and they wanted me to apply for it. In the summer months, when the college kids were gone, I would be able to work with them processing books to be shelved during the day. Just maybe the Lord would let me go back to work. I prayed about it, and I did not feel any objections from the Lord. I went and applied. I got the job.

10

ANSWERED PRAYER

My hours as night shift supervisor at the library were going to be 5:00 p.m. to 12:00 a.m. when the library closed. I still had to make a walk through the four-story library before I could leave, to make sure no one was left behind studying or hiding out to do mischief after everyone was gone. I had to check every restroom and room that had a door the students could get in. This meant I would get out after midnight and have a thirty-two-mile drive home by myself. Some of the guys at the college, told me, "If anything happens close to the college you call us, and we will come help you. If closer to home you call your husband." The drive was praying time for me over the situations the young people at the college would come and ask me to pray for. I always prayed asking the Lord to not let anything happen on the drive back and forth. If anything had to happen, please let it happen when I was at home. One morning I got up to go shopping and there it was, the left rear tire on my car was flat as a pancake. It was fine when I drove home and got there at 1:30 am the night before. I heard, "I answered your prayer." I knew what I had asked Him. I was praising Him; He is so good. He was letting me see that He was taking care of me.

Rodney had continued going to church. I got a call from him one day. "Mom can you come back to speak at my baptism; I got saved? The pastor said, we could have someone come and speak before we are baptized, if we want. I would like for you to come and speak for me." Oh, my goodness. I was so excited. "Yes, I would love to."

When I hung up the phone, I was crying and praising the Lord. I came to Chicago, because the Lord had made it plain, He wanted me to, and He answered my prayer for my son's soul to be His. I packed a bag and headed out early Saturday morning to go back to Detroit. I was learning the route pretty well by now. God had taken my fear of traveling alone away. I thanked Him for it every time I got in the car to go any distance alone. I knew He was right there with me, and He would take care of me. If anything did happen, He would be there to help me. He was all-powerful sovereign God. I stayed with Rod at his place until early Monday morning before heading back to Chicago. I did not have to be at work until Monday evening, and I should have plenty of time to get back. When I left, unlike the other times, I knew my son was in God's hands.

I had, by this time, read my Bible from cover to cover several times. I had learned to meditate on the Lord and talked to Him all the time. I was alone a lot, but not really. I had the Lord, and He had me. I had a five-hour trip back home and thought about how the Lord works in our lives engineering the circumstances to bring about His purposes. The scripture, *(Samuel 1: 6, The Lord brings death and gives life, CBS)*, came to mind. God had already talked to me about this with Bob's death. He is in control when it is our time to leave this earth. He is in control of when He brings eternal life to us. He freed me up from taking care of Dominic so when the time came, I could take care of mom. Rod started going to church with me while I spent the three months at Mother's house. He heard God's word, and I talked to him about the Lord during that time. God answered my prayer to save Rod's soul. *Isaiah 55: 8 & 9 came to me. (8. "For My thoughts are not your thoughts, and your ways are not My ways." This is the Lord's declaration. 9. "For as heaven is higher than earth, so My ways are higher than your ways, and My thoughts than your thoughts." CSB).* Thinking back who would have ever thought things would work out this way? Follow the Lord long enough and you stop trying to guess what might happen next. Things would get sad, and even scary at times, but I would keep straining to see Him through the clouds. I know without a doubt He was there.

Working in the library in the evenings I was able to get to know many of the students. The Lord had me in a position where the students who had problems come up in their lives, would come over to the library to talk to me. We could pray together. Many of the students were missionary kids whose parents were still serving in other counties. These students did not have anyone around to talk to in person other than their own peers. Students, from the music department, filled a car with students and their instruments and came for church Sunday mornings to play for us. We would have them in for dinner after the service. They had a chance to get home cooking once a week. A welcome change from cafeteria food every other day. The church loved having the students and would make dishes of food to help me feed all the kids each Sunday. I had a piano at the house, and the kids would stay just about all afternoon and play the piano, singing and enjoying being in a home atmosphere. Family came in once in a while, but we enjoyed the activity and laughter the kids brought.

11

NOT FOR GOD, NOT GOING TO HAPPEN

This was the time when there started being a big fuss about contemporary music or hymns in the church. This seemed to be an issue in the churches where we ministered or visited. I decided that I was not going to play the piano for the church. The music seemed to be keeping a division in the churches from up North down to where we were. I thought, "I do not want to get in the middle of all this." I was raised with arguing and fussing a great deal of the time, and I certainly did not want the fussing coming at me because I played the piano. I liked most songs from the hymn book, gospel music and contemporary music. Music from all these genres touched my heart. Some of the people in the church were telling about how the authors of the old hymns wrote those songs through suffering. It was their trials and suffering that brought the songs from their souls. This was true. We had singing groups in to sing specials in our churches and I had learned that when talking with these people, that they also have been through many tragedies, like many of the old hymn writers. Song writers today, as well as the old-time hymn writers, have testimonies that bring tears to a person's eyes. My heart goes out to these song writers and singers of our music of today when I get to listen to them tell what motivated them write some of their songs. I don't think there is anything that kills the Spirit of God's moving on a church faster than people walking out of a service grumbling and complaining about the music or their pastor. What I saw was Satan using music to try and bring division in the church, and it was working pretty well. All the arguing over the music in the church was another prayer to keep lifting up before the Lord.

I was not attending classes anymore at the college during the day. With working evenings, I thought I would start piano lessons again so that I could play for my own enjoyment. I found a place to take lessons and started taking lessons again. After a couple of months of taking piano lessons, I noticed something strange happening. Whenever I sat down to practice or go for my lessons, my hands would start shaking. It got so bad, I stopped taking piano lessons. I did not shake any other time. What was wrong with me? In prayer one morning, I asked God, "What is going on? Why am I shaking so badly when I try to play the piano?" While I was working in my flower beds later that day, I heard, "If you do not play for me, you will not play at all." What I had told the Lord before I started taking piano lessons came to mind. I had told

Him that if He would let me play the piano, I would play for the church. This was another lesson learned. Don't tell the Lord you are going to do something for His glory and not carry through with it. He does not forget, even though we may.

I still have the piano I bought from a music shop in Canada. It is a black, ebony upright that I have to remind me, every time I dust it, that you do not say, "No" to what God wants you to do. I thought I had the piano sold once. The guy paid for a piano tuner to come out and check it out to make sure it was what I said it was. The day before he came, he rechecked what he had written down about the piano and realized he was wanting a higher upright piano. When anyone comes, who can play a piano, I have them sit down and play it so I can hear it. I have forgotten all I learned and lost all desire to play. I realized God was in it, and I might as well keep it and dust it, and consider it a lesson well learned. I must say, it holds up pictures, and they look good on it. It also looks pretty when I decorate it for the holidays.

12

GOD SPEAKS

Before I knew it, I got a call from Marc letting me know Missy was in labor, and that they were headed for the hospital. I had my bags packed; I knew the time was close. I jumped into the car and headed out for the long drive back to Marc and Missy's in Mt Pleasant, Michigan. I had to drive through Gary, Indiana, and wouldn't you know, I hit a traffic jam. It that took me two hours to drive three miles. I was praying, talking all the way to the Lord. I finally got to the hospital; my first grandson Andrew had just been born. The doctor sent Marc with the baby to be cleaned up, and I stayed with Missy waiting for the after birth to deliver.

Little Andrew was not to excited too come into this world. It had been a rough delivery, and Missy was wearing out. The doctor had worked for quite some time to get Andrew delivered short of taking Missy for a C-section. I sat beside my daughter talking with the doctor. He would wait a few minutes and then would try to get the afterbirth to break loose. No matter what he did, it would not come loose. Missy was getting really worn out from all the trauma to her body, and the doctor was wearing out, too, from all that he had to do. Finally, the doctor said he was going to take Missy to the operating room and get it out. I heard the Lord speak to me, "Pray that I loosen it." I had been praying for the Lord to please help Missy, but when He speaks, it is a command as to what to pray exactly. I said to the doctor, "First, do you mind if I pray over my daughter?" He rolled back away a little bit motioning me to go ahead and pray. I put my hand on her stomach and prayed out loud for the Lord to release the afterbirth. I thanked the Lord and told the doctor to try one more time. He did what I told him to do, and by the way he looked at me when he went back in after the afterbirth, I knew something had happened. He said, "It just fell into my hand." I said, "Doctor, you just saw my God work a miracle."

The doctor was stunned when he saw this miracle. The doctor canceled the operating room. God did what He told me to tell the doctor to do. I was beginning to pay attention. When God gives me the specific words to pray, I know He will do what He telling me to pray. I have noticed when He comes like this to give me the words to pray, I am so caught up in the situation that I am not thinking to pray. So, I know it's the Holy Spirit directing me, not my thought inspiring me to pray. How He has complete control over my life, never ceases to amaze me.

Missy and the baby were supposed to go home the next day, but after such a rough delivery, the doctor told us that she would have to stay in the hospital a couple of days. God had other plans. By the next day, no one could believe how much better Missy was. She could eat and was able to get up and walk; she had color back in her face. They did not think she would be able to walk for a day or so. She was released the next day after having Andrew in the afternoon the day before. So, baby and mama both came home. I stayed on a little while to help her with the new baby. On my way home, the Lord brought to my mind how I was so upset I would not make it to the hospital on time. The Lord let me know that He is always on time. It may not be our time, but it is in His. He had me there when it was most important. I was there for Him to pray through me to order the afterbirth to be released. God only works when His people pray. Like I said before, I was learning His lessons for real in my life. It was more than reading about them in books or the Bible. I read about them and am learning to pay attention to recognize when my Lord's hand is at work around and in my life.

I was working the afternoon shift at the college library and was home one morning, when my husband got a call from a guy's wife from the church. Her husband Erwin was sick, and the doctor had put Erwin on hospice at his home. This was very early in the morning; we were not dressed yet for the day. Erwin's wife was on the phone, "Please come as soon as possible; Erwin has taken a turn for the worse." She had called the hospice nurse, and after talking to her, she called her family and us to come as soon as possible. We only lived about four blocks away, and by the time we got dressed and to Erwin's house the hospice nurse was going in the door ahead of us. Erwin was in a coma; he was breathing with a death rattle. We could see the tracks on his legs and ankles that come when the body starts shutting down. After praying over Erwin, we went back into the kitchen and talked with Erwin's wife while the nurse was checking Erwin's vitals. Family members started coming in. The nurse said it would not be long, and he would not be with us any longer. Erwin was in a hospital bed in front of a picture window in the living room. We stayed in the back of the living room, so when his family came in they had plenty of room to be near him until he passed.

It had been about an hour after the nurse left, and all their children had finally made it to the house to be with their mom and dad. Shortly after the last one got there, and they were all standing around the bed; Erwin opened his eyes. He became as alert as any of us and started talking. The rattle in his breathing was gone. He called each one of his kids to come up close to him and proceeded to tell each of them what they needed to give up or do to get themselves right with the Lord. I do not know if he had ever talked to them in such a way before. He came down pretty hard on some of them. When he got done talking to them, we heard Erwin say, "Pastor, Come over here." We did not even know he knew we were in the room. He had been in a coma when we came. We had tried to be quiet and let the family have the last few minutes with their father. My husband jumped up and went to the bedside. Erwin wanted him right up close. Erwin than said, "Pastor, you feed my sheep." My husband said he would. Erwin closed his eyes and took his last breath. There was not a person in that room who had any doubt that it was the Lord speaking through Erwin that day. Some of Erwin's children were told they better get in church. He told others, who were in church what they better quit doing, if they were going to be pleasing in God's sight. Erwin's children took their father's words seriously. We saw the miracle through Erwin, and we saw the changes that came in his children. I had heard of God working in such ways, but that day we witnessed it first-hand. When a person gives his all to the Lord, God will show Himself, often in unexpected ways.

If God disciplines me or blesses me, I am blessed either way. He is still talking to me and He does what He does because He loves me. I cry and repent when I disappoint Him, but praise Him for caring enough to talk to me and change me. God loved Erwin's children enough to speak to them in such a way they knew it was God speaking. God cares about us and our children.

At the college library, I was getting acquainted with those who worked behind the scenes. I only knew the ladies who shelved books or worked behind the checkout counter, before I started working in the library. I knew no one who worked behind the scenes. Not long after I started work, I would get called to see if I would be willing to go in early and fill in when someone was sick or off in behind-the-scenes departments. My job was coming to an end during summer break. I was praying, "Lord, what can I do?" He answered my prayer. Because I was willing to go in early and help fill in where they needed help, I was able to work in the processing department during the summer, and when the students were off for breaks. This kept me working full time. I was so grateful.

I was praising the Lord, for I knew He was making this all possible.

As I spent a lot of time alone, and it seemed the prayer list was long, I was still able to spend plenty of alone time with the Lord. We lived close to the church. There was only one house between our house and the church. I would still go to the church to pray every morning. For the first time, I worked in a Christian setting at the library with women who were all believers. Not all were Nazarenes, but all were believers. That was wonderful. I was privileged to meet some prayer warriors at work. We would pray for each other's needs. There were many times I needed prayer, and I did not feel I could go to anyone in our church. I was not getting hives from speaking in front of people anymore, but the stress I had at home was causing the hives now. The Lord provided believers who would help me pray.

13

NEXT MOVE

When my husband got his degree in preaching, he was ready to move on to another church. I was not sad about leaving the crazy Chicago life, but hated leaving the students and all the people I had made friends with at the church. I did not understand why we had to keep moving, but I knew the Lord was in it. He is in everything. I did not fight the Lord this time; I proceeded to get boxes and started packing.

Since we had left the farm, we had lived in houses the churches provided for their pastor and families. Our next move would mean we would have to find our own place to live. My husband accepted an inner-city church in Springfield, Illinois. This move was about eight hours from my family. With buying our own house we did not have to live right in the city. We could get out a little bit.

Do you remember me telling you I had rented out my mother's home just in case I ever needed it? Well,

I needed to sell it so we could buy our own house. I called the realtor who was taking care of the house for me. Because I was living hours away from my mother's house, the realtor took care of the headaches that can come along with renting. The realtor told me that he was getting ready to call me. The man renting my mother's house loved it there and wanted to buy her house, if I would be willing to sell it. I knew the Lord was in the move. Only God could arrange such a thing with such perfect timing.

I started praying to the Lord to show us where He wanted us to live. I asked Him to make it clear to me what He wanted for us. This picture came to my mind: a house with a red brick sidewalk leading to the front door, and an open staircase at the front door leading to an upstairs. I shared this with my husband. We went out for a day with a realtor looking at places. I was getting to the point where none of the houses seemed to be right for us. Finally, the realtor lady said, "I have one last place that might work, but it's a little further out." We went to look at it. The first thing I saw as we approached, was a two-story home. We drove in the driveway and there was the red brick sidewalk. I knew when the realtor opened the front door there was going to be the staircase I had envisioned. Yes, there it was. It was perfect. We had the spare bedrooms for family to come and stay with us and a bedroom for an exchange student from Argentina who would be coming shortly after we moved in.

We were in a subdivision, but everyone had one or two acres. I could have a garden, and there was breathing room. There were woods behind the house; and at the bottom edge, a little trickling stream that ran through it. I did not know that this little wooded area would come to be a treasured spot on the place for me one day. The house had a bedroom downstairs with a bathroom right next to it for our parents to stay when they came and spent time. Both of our parents were able to drive but climbing stairs would have been a problem. This was perfect.

When in our last church, several of the people had adopted children or taken in teens from other countries to come live with their family in America. My husband decided he wanted to adopt a child. Everyone made a fuss over the families with these adopted babies. Under the circumstances I was not about to adopt, I was in my fifties. I did agree to take in a student for a year. So, in addition to moving, I had to make arrangements with the school system to sign up a young man who was a senior in high school to attend school in the fall. When I called to make the arrangements, they put me in touch with the school Superintendent.

When I was talking to the school Superintendent, I don't know what came over me. I asked, "Oh, by the way, you would not have a job opening, would you?" He said, "As a matter of fact I do. I need a para-pro at the elementary school not five miles from where you live. It is a full-time position." I could not believe that God was opening doors all over the place. The Lord was making it very clear to me that this was where we were supposed to be.

As it turned out, the Lord was not wanting us to adopt children. He had something else worked out that was going to bring lots of children into my life. I did not know it, but I would be working with children who would be challenged in so many ways. Prayer was going to be so greatly needed for myself and for the kids. We barely got unpacked enough to find our clothes when we picked up the young man from Argentina. Marcello was going to live with us for a year. We were given information on him; however, you do not really know an exchange student, until he/she gets in your home. He was not a believer; his parents owned a school and were wealthy. Marcello was used to servants waiting on him and had the attitude, we found out later, that he was coming to America to party and have a good time. I pray all the prayers that went up for him worked somewhere along in his life. His brother was in college here in America and came to spend a few days with us a couple of times. He was a totally different young man. He would apologize for Marcello's attitude.

Here I was going to school again. I did not know what an adventure I was in for. I was given a little girl no one wanted. She had down syndrome, was autistic and psychotic. She also had three other diagnoses. This little ten-year-old girl had so many challenges. The first week she had locked herself in the principal's office and in a bathroom stall, and I had to crawl under the door to get her out. Another time the principal and I had to run as fast as we could down the middle of the road in front of the school to catch her. When we went out for recess, and it crossed her mind that she did not want to go back in for class, she would wrap herself around a pole on the swings or slides and hang on for dear life. It took the principal and someone else to help me get her back into the building.

I really started praying for the Lord to show me what I might be able to do to get her interested in learning. How could I make it a game for Tori? I love arts and crafts, so I started getting pictures in my mind of things to make to help her learn. I started making all kinds of posters and games to help her relate to the different topics. Tori did not work well in a group setting, so we were given an area by ourselves to work in. I prayed lots of prayers pleading for God to help me and open her little mind to want to learn. I saw God begin to answer my prayers. What God had shown me to make for her, was making a difference in Tori, and she began to enjoy learning. He did what I had asked Him to do. What I made seemed more like games to her. We stopped seeing so much of the bad behavior. I was praising the Lord. Some of my co-workers would see what I had made and ask me where I bought the material Tori was working with. I told them that the Lord showed me what to make, and I made it. They told me I needed to get a patent on it. It could help children like Tori learn. I didn't. I did not feel that was what the Lord wanted me to do.

Tori's behavior was really changing; she was beginning to listen to me and actually like me. The principal and staff at the school noticed, and so did her parents at home. Her mom asked me one day if I had ever considered doing respite work? I had never heard too much about it. When we were in the Upper Peninsula, we had done some Hospice work. That work involved going into the homes, and reading to the patients, staying with them for a couple hours to give the care giver a break. Tori's mom told me that they had thirty hours of respite work a week, and they needed someone who would take Tori.

Tori was changing, so I checked into what respite was all about. I found out that there would be ten weeks of classes for both myself and my husband to attend, even though he would not be the one responsible for the children that I may be caring for. He wanted the money, so he agreed. I started having Tori thirty hours a week, most of the time from Friday nights to Saturday night or through Sundays. She loved the dogs, and this is where the woods behind the woods came in. We would take the dogs and head for the woods as soon as her mother left. She would play and run until she was exhausted. I did with her like I did with my kids. She helped me cook and garden. She was right beside me. She often would cry when she had to go home. I got to see the Lord work wonders in that little girl. The next year she moved on, and I would never see her again.

The end of the school year came for Marcello. He did not apply himself. He thought that since he was in another country he did not have to. When it came time for graduation, his brother came and spent a few more days with us and attended Marcello's graduation with me. Marcello's brother went to the school to talk with administrators to see how his brother had done. Marcello was in for a shock. He had planned on coming back to the United States to go to college like his brother was doing. His brother told Marcello that he did not get good enough grades to get into a college in the United States; he would have to stay in their home country to go to college. It was a great day of awaking for Marcello, but it was too late. He had squandered his time, and now he would pay for it.

14

INNER CITY CHURCH

eantime, we were at an inner-city church in Springfield, Ill. The Lord was going to show me how much He had changed my heart when it came to people who did drugs and alcohol. In our ministry, we encountered recovered drug addicts and alcoholics, those in the process of recovering, and those who wanted to recover. What we saw broke our hearts. We picked up kids to bring them into church. The things we would be told would make me want to cry. Two little girls that we picked up were in my Sunday school class. After they began to get to know me, they started telling me what went on at home. Their mom made them sit in a chair and watch TV while she entertained men in her bedroom. Another young boy in his teens would come up missing for a couple of days. He finally told us what was going on when he came up missing. His mom was single, and they did not have much money so he would sell himself on the streets. The guys who would pick him up would get him high on drugs, and then he did not care what they did to him as long as he got his money.

I got to know a little girl who was about thirteen years old. She was brought to church by the church van. It was getting close to Thanksgiving, and I remember asking her what her family was going to do for the holiday. I found out it was just her and her dad. Her dad had both legs amputated, and she took care of him. Her mother had packed up and walked out on both of them. She did not know where her mother was. She had wanted to have a turkey, but she did not know if they could get one. We let some people in the church know, and we got them a Thanksgiving meal put together like I don't think that little girl had ever seen. We found out where she lived and took it to her house. We discovered that her dad slept on a mattress on the floor by the front door so he could roll out of the house quickly, if he needed too. The house was so dirty and nasty, and I helped her clean the stove and refrigerator and the kitchen. I did not want to take the food into the house until there was a clean place to put it. I told her how to warm up what needed to be warmed some. Most things were prepared for her. The church always made sure after that, when we had pot lucks, we packed up the left-over food and sent it home with her.

It always amazed me that these people who had gone to church all their lives did not understand how to pray. I assumed that people are in church because they want to be Holy, love the Lord and grow more pleasing to Him. It is sad to learn this is not always so. Some people do not understand that it is about a relationship with the Lord that is going to get them into heaven. The Christian life is not just showing up to church when the doors are open. I guess that is why that in every church we ever served, the Lord led me to take the women through Hinthorn's four study books. The books taught people to pray. I was learning not to assume because people had been in church most of their lives, that they knew how to live a life that was pleasing to the Lord. There are people who think if they get their bodies inside a church once a week, they are good with the Lord.

I started an evening Bible study with a group of ladies. I was learning that there are people who do not think they should pray for themselves. A couple of ladies told me they thought it was a selfish thing to do. They thought they were supposed to pray for others and everything else, but not themselves. This is nothing but a lie from Satan. We are to pray for God to search us, and make us more like Him. We are to pray for things that will bring glory to our Lord. One lady in particular stands out in my mind. Fannie and her husband had been in church for years. She told me she never prayed for herself. This couple was up in their 70's and none of their children were believers. When she began to learn how to pray, she prayed for God to search her and change things in her life that were not pleasing to Him. Then she began to see changes. Not only was she seeing God making changes in herself, but God was answering her prayers, and their children began coming to church.

Fannie was not the only one changing. In our church, testimonies at any time were welcome. Women began to stand up and testify as to what the Lord was doing in their lives and families. A few months into the study with the women, some of the men from the church came to me and asked me if they could come to the study. I had tried to encourage my husband to have a men's study, but he wouldn't. I told them they would have to ask my husband; He was the pastor, and it would be his decision, not mine. So, they did. They all went to him at the same time. He didn't tell them they couldn't. He was not thrilled about it, but he told them it was ok. I didn't care who is in the studies; I just wanted people to learn. Souls depended on it.

I would come straight from working at the school to the church for the study. When I would get to the church, the guys would have the coffee on and donuts or something to snack on when I walked in the door. Those men were more consistent than some of the women. They wanted to grow. They had studied their lesson and were ready to go.

I did not know it at the time, but the Lord was putting finishing touches on two of the women to prepare them to come home to be with Him. Fannie was praising the Lord each time she saw her children walk in the church, and at times her kids would be at the altar seeking the Lord. Fannie's husband was one who insisted on coming to the Bible study with Fannie. He saw her grow spiritually, and he saw her prayers being answered for their family. One day we got a call. Fannie's husband was going to run to the store for Fannie, and she had walked with him out on their back deck to see him off. He got in the car and looked back to see Fannie on the deck. He called an ambulance and the family. We got the call and rushed to the hospital. We found out Fannie had a heart attack. We were there when she went to be with Jesus. She got to see her prayer answered before the Lord took her home. She went in peace. Fannie had learned to pray.

The other lady was Joyce, the church secretary. She had a bad back and was on prescription pain medicine for her back. She had become addicted to the pills, and when she learned to start praying for herself, she shared with my husband and me that the Lord spoke to her, He wanted her to get off of the medicine. Joyce had become badly addicted to the medication. She had to get through withdrawal from the medicine, but she did not want to have to go to a hospital or anywhere else. She asked us to help her. We did; we stayed with her and prayed for her, took care of her, and I kept reading what the Lord brought to me to read to her. Satan does not let go easily, and thank the Lord, He had given me the grace to be able to be with people who were terribly sick and not get sick myself. Joyce made it through the withdrawal process and was back in church to tell her testimony of how the Lord had spoken to her. It was not easy, but He brought her through. A few months later He came for Joyce. She passed quickly. There was no doubt in anyone's mind that the Lord was preparing these ladies to be with Him.

This church had come through a terrible split just before we got there, but the people who remained stood strong with the Lord and wanted to grow. The church owned property across from the existing church, and about a year after we were there, they decided to build a new sanctuary on the vacant property. The church had several men who had the skills to build, so the church got built by the hands of its members. We women pitched in and helped. Working at the school, I had my summer off, so I was free to be there quite a bit. I loved building; my first husband and I built our first home, and we doing most of the work ourselves.

15

TIME FOR SCHOOL AGAIN

Summer was over and it was time to go back to school again. The school superintendent called to tell me, that there was not a position for me at the school I had worked at the year before because, but there was a position at a school a few miles further away. I know it was the grace of God, *(remember I do not believe in chance)* that the guy who drove the van that picked up the special need's children lived in the same subdivision that we did. As a matter of fact, He lived just two houses down from ours. He was retired and liked getting out a couple times a day. Driving the van gave him something to do. This man would pick me up first and then the boy Kevin. I would be taking care of Keven all day at the school and he lived in the subdivision right across the road from ours. Kevin would be the first one on the van in the morning. Then we would drive to the other children's homes to load them on. The other children's para-pros would meet us at the van when we pulled into the school parking lot to take their children to class. Kevin would be there with me. They needed two people on the van to pick up the kids and it would work out perfectly if I would be willing to ride the van morning and night. I said I would be glad to.

This time I was going to get a ten-year-old boy, Kevin. He was a normal-looking boy, but his mother told me about Kevin. When Kevin was born it was discovered that he was missing a protein gene. He was a ten-year-old with an eight-month-old mentality. Kevin could not walk, feed himself, talk or do anything for himself. He was an eight-month-old in a ten-year-old body. The Lord was leading me into another challenge, I was going to need His help. God was teaching me to pray about every-thing all day long. At home, at work, everywhere were challenges, and I needed Him to give me the grace and wisdom to make it through.

Kevin was basically a happy little boy, and he had wonderful parents. When he was happy, he would squeal and giggle, and when he did not want to do something, he would cry and scream. Up to this point no one had done much with Kevin at school. The Lord laid it on my heart to teach Kevin to walk. There was a walker there for him. He did not want to walk, so he would scream, and the para-pros would stop working with him. I started praying about this and telling the Lord, that because He brought Kevin to me, He must want to do something with him. He had to show me. I could go wherever I wanted with these children, so I put Kevin in his wheel chair, grabbed his walker and off to the cafeteria we went. It was off at a distance from classrooms so that where if

Kevin screamed, it would not bother anyone. I pushed him there, and we went in to talk with the ladies who worked there preparing food. I told them I was going to work with Kevin to teach him to walk. I asked them if Kevin's squealing and screaming would bother them. Kevin had been in that school from his first day of school, and the women were excited that he might learn to walk. All the ladies told me that it would be just fine for me to work with Kevin in the cafeteria. So, I prayed and told the Lord He had to do what only He could do, and we proceeded to work with Kevin. I got Kevin out of the wheel chair, stood behind him, and put his hands on the walker, holding his hands there with mine. With my feet sliding his feet each step of the way, Kevin began his new journey. We did this twice a day starting out slowly, and building up more time as each week went by. At first Kevin would scrunch up his face, look at me and scream. I would tell him; "It's going to be okay, we are going to do it anyway," and I kept him moving on.

Parts of Kevin's day would be in a regular classroom with the other kids in his grade. He did not understand, but he liked being with the kids watching them, and they liked talking to him. One day a little girl brought me a wrapped-up gift. I could tell she had wrapped up the gift herself. When she handed it to me, I asked her, "What is this for?" Her answer was not at all what I expected, and it broke my heart. She told me, "I wanted to bring you something for being so nice to Kevin. The other ladies were mean to him." The kids saw how Kevin was being treated. I was shocked. I took her treasure she gave me, thanked her and gave her a hug. We always sat at group

131

tables, and the teachers always appreciated the extra help I could be with all the children who sat with Kevin and me. I loved working with the other kids, as well as Kevin.

Kevin's mom came for every activity that parents were invited to participate in. She would come early, find Kevin and me, and we would talk. It did not take long for Kevin to get the hang of walking, and we could walk the halls of the school without him fussing about it. She came early one day when there was going to be a party. When she started down the hall there was Kevin walking with his walker. I was still right behind him but did not have to be holding on to his hands anymore or move his feet for him. She could not believe her eyes. She was seeing her son walk for the first time. When she got over her excitement, she told me that she could see Kevin building muscle tone in his legs, but could not imagine what I was doing with him to make this happen. I shared with her that the Lord was leading me how to teach Kevin to walk and use his hands to hold on to the walker. I told her we needed to praise the Lord. This was His work, not mine. When she found out I was licensed for respite care, she asked if I would take care of Kevin in my home when she needed help.

The Lord had made it clear to me, that what I was doing was His will. He had put me in a situation in which I had not a clue what to do. If He wanted me to do something, He would have to give me clear directions. I would do what He said, and watch to see what He was going to do. He did not disappoint me. All the glory was His. On days Kevin would be sick, I did not have to stay home. I still rode the van to pick up the kids and stayed at the school working those days helping in the school library. I got to read stories to the children or worked on shelving books. The Lord never wastes the talents He has given us, if we are willing to use them.

I was still cutting hair for people in the church. At women's retreats I would cut hair for a money donation. Then the money would go to a pastor and family who might need it in the district. There would be several children that we bused in to our churches from very poor households. I would send a note and get written permission to cut these kids' hair at no charge. Kids are mean to each other at school, and at least I could help by cutting these kid's hair. I would cut hair for people who were sick for a prolonged amount of time. I always had a basket with my cape, clippers, and scissors in the back of my car to cut hair where ever I might be.

We had been at this place a little over two years, and I had been able to go through the school year with Kevin. The new church was almost completed, and my husband decided he wanted to move again. He was looking for a bigger church.

16

MORE BOXES

We had been moving about every two to three years, each move further way from my home in Michigan. I was becoming an expert on packing. I was beginning to feel like I did when I was a child, and my dad a welder/pipe fitter, moved us after each job was done. We moved constantly until I was a teenager. That was why I was so determined to stay in one place when I grew up and had a place of my own. I was staying put. Now I realize that the Lord had other plans for my life. He did bless me to be able to stay in one place until my kids were able to be out on their own before He put me on the move again.

This move was not going to be so bad; we were going east this time to Louisville, Kentucky, horse country. The Lord let us know He was in it; the house sold the first week it was on the market. I liked the house and wished I could pack it up and move it too. We drove across to interview for the church. The district superintendent we had in Northern Michigan had moved to this district. We knew him and his wife. The District Office was there at the church we were going to be going to. We at least knew someone when we went there.

So here I was driving a U-Haul following a U-Haul, and again asking the Lord what was up. This answer was going to take a few more years to get.

I was not given any idea what to be looking for as far as a house that He would have for us, even though I was asking God to show me. We looked at houses after houses until again, like before, they all began to run in together. All that seemed to be for sale were homes in subdivisions all packed in so close. We found a house being built in a new section of a subdivision that only had a couple of homes in it. There were none next to this one house that was almost complete. A couple had started it, and then were getting a divorce and did not want the house. We ended up buying it. By the time we would be making the move it would be completed on the inside. Just some work would need to be done on the outside. This place turned out to be a disaster. We moved in. When a person walked up to the front door, there was a window on the outside for the bathroom right there by the front door. When you walked into the bathroom, there was no window. That had to be redone. Louisville has torrential rains. The first rain that came after we moved into our home caused flooding in the garage. The fire alarms started going off, and I did not know how to stop them. Come to find out the valleys on the roof of the house did not have any flashing under the shingles. The big window in the front bedroom upstairs had to be totally replaced. The basement had a door that led out into the back yard. Because there was no drain at the bottom of the stairs going down to the basement, the basement would flood when it rained.

My husband was gone most of the time, and I had to deal with getting all these repairs taken care of. Worker were all around our subdivision as more houses were being built there. I like baking cookies and always had a container full of them. When the workers came, I always had all the cookies they wanted and something to drink for them. At least I did not have to wait for the guys to come. They were always ready for cookies. The Lord would answer that prayer quickly.

Our church treasurer at our Louisville church was also on the school board in Louisville, Kentucky. When she found out I had worked in schools, she said she would speak for me to get into the school system there. A person pretty much had to know someone to get in. I went and applied thinking I was applying for a full-time position like I had in the last place. I found out it would only be-full time part-time job working with the children of the adults taking adult education classes. We lived on the South end of Louisville, and I would be working two days a week having to drive over to the West-side and two nights a week at a place about half way between my place and the day job. I was advised to take it because it would get my foot in the door to move up later when an opening came in the regular school system.

I was given the address to be there where I was supposed to show up for work and time, but did not know what was expected of me to do. I knew only that I would be working with the students' children. "Lord help me," was my constant prayer. I was told by people at the church to keep my doors locked and move quickly from my car to the building. I was not to linger outside. Later, I added to my prayer, "Please Lord, let my car be out there when I get ready to go home." Not too long after starting these two jobs, I had a third location added to my week. On the night jobs, I had children of school age who I helped with their homework. I had to prepare things for them to do if they did not have homework. I could do this. The day job was a little different. I had from a six-week-old baby to kindergarten age children. On the night jobs there would usually be two of us working with the kids. I was supposed to have help with the day job, but it seemed the helpers would show up a few times and then we did not see them again. If the main office could spare someone to come help me, they would send them over at these times, but I was alone a lot of the time with about twelve children. The Lord helped me. I had a six-week-old baby and all these toddlers. Thank goodness, I had a gym I could take them to full of toys. I would have them get in a line and make a game of marching to the gym.

I worked at these jobs until an opening came at an elementary school about five miles from where I lived. I had gotten to know the moms of the little ones from the day school job, because, for the most part, the kids and I were in an adjoining room. They came in, had snack time with their kids, and the new mom could check on her baby anytime she felt she wanted to. Some of these students lived in their cars, they were a tough group of people. I heard some stories at this place. I was so thankful that the

Lord was with me and the students liked me. When the students learned I would be leaving to work full time in an elementary school closer to my home, they were sad I was leaving but happy for me. My last day I did not know it, but they had planned a good bye party for me.

I will have to tell you here, the day before my last day, during snack time when the moms who were in the room with me and their children. Another mom went over and put her hand on the baby who was asleep in a crib. The baby's mom did not like this lady too much. I did not know there was a feud going on between these two women.

The next day when I walked in, all the students were waiting for me and had made some decorations and a card for me. They wanted to wish me well as I went on to my next job. The teacher had helped them to make some decorations and a card for me with a picture of a horse glued on, because they knew I loved horses. It made me cry. They did not know that my tears were because they cared so much for me, and that it meant so much to me that they would do this for me. The teacher told them, that the tears were because I cared for them and their children, and it touched me that they cared for me enough to do this for me. This was not an emotion these people were used too. These people were raised in the streets and emotions were lost to them.

I got hugs from them, and they told me sure would miss me. The mom with the baby told me I could take care of her baby anytime. From her that was special.

After the class had left that day, I talked to the teacher a little bit before I left. She told me that the mom who had the baby had planned on coming to school and killing the mom who had touched her baby the day before. Because she thought the world of me, and she did not want to ruin the party for me, she decided not to. I was in shock. I was told that showing so much emotion to me was foreign to this group. I had learned to pray for years that the Lord would hide me and let people see His love through me. I did not have it to give, but I knew He had lots to spread around. He was showing me how He was with me and answering my prayer.

Meantime I had started teaching a Bible study at this church. Some of the women were excited to get a study going. There was one lady Pat who had been a pastor's wife for forty years, and she and her husband started coming there to church about the time we arrived. She was so excited she was going to have her own pastor's wife. She knew my position well, and she was a sweetheart. She was one I could talk to and pray with. I was blessed with a group of ladies hungry for more of the Lord. During the years I was there, we did not have many times we did not meet weekly. I had the privilege of watching so many of these ladies grow.

New houses began being built around our house and the houses were about fifteen feet apart. I could stand in my kitchen window and look from my dining room window into the kitchen of the house next door. When we sat on our back deck, we could hear every word that was spoken by the neighbors sitting on their deck behind us. We did not last but about eight months at this place.

We had gone out for a ride one day exploring the area around where we lived. When we had gone about four miles out further in a more rural area, we saw this house that was on some acreage for sale. We stopped and talked to the lady who was home. She told us that this place was for sale, if the closing on the house they wanted to buy went through. If it did not, the house was going off the market. We had been praying for the Lord show us what to do. I believe the Lord got us out there for a reason. We called the realtor who had the house listed right then from our cell phone and told her we would be interested in it if the other deal went through. She took all our information. Someone came along right behind us interested in the house. It was a miracle we did get the place. As soon as we got the call that the closing for the people who were selling their house was going to happen, we got on the phone to the realtor who happened to be at a party in downtown Louisville. She wrote the information she needed on a napkin and took off for her office. Everything was taken care of quickly, and we got the house and five acres. It was the Lord in it. Even the realtors were amazed when they saw how it all flowed so quickly. What usually takes time took only hours, it seemed, and we were signing papers on the place. The house needed to be painted throughout, but I was going to be out of the subdivision. Thank You Jesus! Our house went up for sale in the subdivision.

We were moving again but did not need any U-Hauls this time. With some help from some of the people from the church we got moved. I loved it here. We had room again. I had a big enough dining area to have the church board out for dinners again. When I was back home in Midland, Michigan, once a month I always had family out to the farm to celebrate whoever ever had a birthday that month. In the ministry we would have the church board and their spouses in for dinner on special occasions. At Christmas we would have an open house on Christmas Eve Day, and the church was invited out between 1:00 p.m. and 6:00 p.m. for finger foods and fellowship with us and each other. People came and went the whole time. We had a yard to where we could host church picnics again. These things were not going to happen in the house in the subdivision, but it was a holding place until this place was going to be available. The Lord's timing is perfect. He put us in the right place to get a house that was better suited to our needs.

17

ANOTHER NEW SCHOOL

The Lord blessed me again. This school was a 10-minute drive from our place. I started out in first grade with a little boy named Kenny. Kenny was considered legally blind. He could see shadows. I had to do all of Kenny's reading and writing for him, as well as, stay by his side all day to get him around. He could not run and play on the playground like the other kids. He really did not interact with the other kids. Kenny was easy to work with being a quiet little boy. The teacher placed a little boy at the table with Kenny and me who did not speak English. So, while I worked with Kenny, I was able to work with this little guy too.

This school had several of us who were believers working there. We began meeting before school in a classroom at the far end of one of the halls for prayer every morning before the children got there. We could share about children who needed prayer, as well as, pray over the school and lift up anyone's personal prayer requests. A few months after that, we found an empty closet storage room, and we started a once-a-week Bible study. We would squeeze in this little room and sit on kids' chairs. We saw so many answers to prayer. We had inner city kids being bussed out to this school. Some of these little guys were tough, and I have no doubt had older siblings that belonged to gangs. We prayed over these kids. I was going to learn that this was going to be totally different from the other schools where I had worked. I was going to have several children to work with at one time. The school assigned me to work with some students, but others the Lord gave me so He could love and nurture through me. I will never drive past a school and look at it in the way I used to. All those little lives in that building have so many stories, some good, some not so good.

Our schools are full of little ones who are made in the image of God, and Satan wants to destroy them before God can open their hearts to serve Him. God loves those little children, and if Satan can destroy those little lives, he can get at God. Satan cannot touch God, so he is bent on destroying God's children. Prayer is as much needed in the school as it is in the church. I was beginning to see how Satan works in our homes. I could see some of this in the church but got a broader view of how Satan works in the family to destroy lives, as I worked for the schools. We see the more obvious when parents are physically abusive to their children, but I was beginning to see how much that lack of discipline is abusive to our kids also. For their own sake they need to be disciplined in love. The Bible tell us, if we love our children, we will discipline them in love. This balance is missing in our homes today, and the rolls have reversed in so many homes. The children are telling the parents what to do. Children are supposed to be a blessing from God to us, and most parents are putting everything else in front of taking time to raise their children the way God, in His Word, instructs parents. When Satan was allowed to take prayer out of our schools by one woman, we were heading for destruction on a faster pace in our country. At least at this school, we found a way to have prayer over these kids and their families.

I loved working with these kids and wanted to learn more so I could help them. I learned that in the summer months they would have classes to teach us to be better equipped to walk through a day with these children. The next summer I took all the classes I could take. I had already walked through a year with Tori which gave me a jump start with children with the same disabilities she had. These classes were going to give me a lot more insight into the way these kids thought. I took classes so I could deal with medical problems like diabetes. I learned to give breathing treatments and how to handle anything that might come up where blood was a problem. I took classes on autism that gave me a little more understanding of what these children had to deal with in their little minds daily.

The next year Kenny's mom got remarried and Kenny moved away, so I was given another little boy. His name was Nick. Nick was in fourth grade and was autistic. Nick's grandmother happened to be Kenny's vison specialist, who came and worked with Kenny once a week.

She helped me know what to do with Kenny. So, when I got Nick, she still came to the school to work with other kids and would always come and talk to me about Nick. When Nick would go to see his doctor for autism, she would always let me know what they discussed. I would talk to the Lord about what I knew and ask Him to give me the wisdom to know what to do to help Nick.

Nick hated to read and write, but that little guy could draw anything, and he was fussy about details. He noticed everything. No one had been able to get Nick to write much. He could spell and fill in words, but he did not want to write sentences. I took it to the Lord for help. One day Nick's grandma mentioned that Nick was sensitive to what he ate concerning texture, and he did not like mint. The assignment came up that the students had to write a little paper. They were assigned to write so many sentences. It came to mind to take several pieces of paper and make it like a little book. I put some lines on the bottom of the page for Nick to write on, but left the top half blank. Nick had a member of the family who had a sailboat that he got to ride in. I gave him the little book I had made and told him to draw me pictures on each page of the sail boat, and what he liked to do on the boat. No problem, he drew me pictures on every page. When he had completed his pictures each day, I got the book out, and I told him he had to write at the bottom three sentences telling what he was doing on one of the pictures.

At first Nick baulked at that. I usually had my jar of Skittles to reward the kids when they did something I would ask them to do. But this time I had hard peppermint candy, and I had him put a piece of candy in his mouth, He could not take it out until he had written three sentences on a page. Then he could take the candy out. Nick started writing, and it would only be a few minutes that he would have his three sentences on a page for a day. I can't believe he did not think to chew it up or spit it out, but he didn't, until I told him he could go to the waste basket each day and spit it out. One day when I got the book out for him to write his sentences on and gave him the candy, he looked at me and said, "Ms. Vicki you are killing me." The other kids at the table said, "Ms. Vicki will you please kill us too?" So, everyone got a mint when it came time to work on their projects. Nick's grandma knew what I was doing, and she could not believe the improvements that Nick was making. When she saw the book that he was making, she was amazed. I had to tell her it was not me, but the Lord working through prayer for Nick.

I got to see up close how God works when His people pray. Another little boy who was brought in from the inner city was in third grade and could not read at all. He came to our table to help me. I had two little boys at my table who could not use their hands or walk. I would have to help these little guys for everything. The Lord impressed on me to talk to the teacher about Shavon. This little guy already had plans for his life, and it did not include being in school. He was sent to the principal's office every day, sometimes more than once. The Lord put it on my mind to work with Shavon to make him feel needed and important. After talking with the teacher, I asked Shavon if he would consider helping me with the kids at my table. Would he come and sit with us, because I needed his help? He was excited about that.

Shavon and I made a deal right away, that each day he was good and did not get into trouble and helped me like he promised, he would get Skittles like the other kids at my table when they accomplished something for me. Each day he did not get sent to the principal's office; I would give him a stick of gum when he was ready to get on the bus. Now, if he could make it all five days without going to the office, on Friday at the end of the day, he would get his stick of gum for the day and a whole pack of five sticks for being good the whole week. At first it was a little rough for him, but when he did not get his gum on those days, when he had to go to the principal's office, he knew I meant it. It was not long when, at the end of each week, he was getting his whole pack of gum. He was learning to read and willing to learn, because he wanted to help those other kids. One Friday I got to work and it dawned on me I was out of gum. I went to the principal and told her I had forgotten to stop at a gas station on my way to work and get more gum. She said, "I will send someone to cover for you. You go get whatever you need."

The Lord knows everyone's needs, and as I kept each one lifted up in prayer, He would reveal to me what to do to help these children.

I was given one little boy, Jordan, needed me to be by his side every minute he was at school. Jordan was like a walking time bomb, ready to explode at any minute. He was a brittle diabetic. His blood sugar levels would go from fifty or lower or off the meter at five hundred in a heartbeat. I guess this is where the sensitivity the Lord gave me with all my animals was helpful with this little guy. I seemed to be able to sense when things were going wrong in his body. I had to have a test kit with him constantly. When his sugar started going up or down, I noticed his behavior start changing, and it was time to test the sugar.

I was soon to learn Jordan came from a very dysfunctional home. His dad married a lady with two little girls who came to school with Jordan. They would tell me what went on at home with the step mom and Jordan. Jordan ate breakfast at school every day, as most of the kids did. On days that Jordan would wake up with low sugar, she would stuff him full of candy bars and send him to school. Other days, if she was mad at him, the girls would tell me that she would not allow him to eat breakfast when he got to school. One day when he came to school his sugar was so bad, we had to call and have him taken to the hospital. She came into the school, down to the room where I was, in a rage, wanting to know what I was doing to her son. She was going to the principal's office and get me fired.

I expected a call to come from the office for me to come down there. No call came from the office. When I got a break, I went down and walked into the principal's office and asked, "Well, do I still have a job?" The principal looked at me and said, "Don't you worry, we know her and your job is safe." We had been instructed that if we saw or expected any abuse, we were to use the school's phones and report it. We would not have to give our names. In time I went and made that call. The only time I went to the phone and made such a call was when I thought Jordan's step mother was mistreating him. Jordan's step sisters told me their mom did not like Jordan. I am not sure, but I think she would have gotten rid of him through his diabetes if she could have. I had a teacher friend who I still am in touch with all these years after leaving the school system, call and tell me about a year after I left, that the courts finally removed Jordan out of the house. I sure prayed he would get in a place where he would be cared for and safe.

I was beginning to see in my life what I was reading about the Lord: God has chosen to work through His chosen one's prayers. If we do not pray, God does not work. He has to be invited in. I don't think many children in our schools have anyone to pray for them. God has access to work in students' when a group of teachers will start praying for them. The thing of it is, Satan slips in, and no one pays any attention, because they are so caught up in their own lives. Many people think it's no big deal to take prayer out of school. Look at the shape our world is in now in 2021 due to the lack of prayer in school.

The Lord put us back on a little acreage so that we could have horses. There was a building we turned into a little barn. We bought two Paso Fino riding horses, and my daughter gave us two miniature horses. When I had the farm with many animals, schools, scouts and day cares would call me to see if they could bring the children out to see the animals. The Lord brought people from all over the area to my beauty shop, and when they saw all the animals, they told others. I always enjoyed sharing what God had blessed me with. I would bake cookies for a treat to give the kids in these different groups before they left.

We used the horses with kids at the church. For Bible School, we hauled the horses in to the church and gave rides to the kids who attended. After the first night and the kids went home and told others about the animals. We had kids coming from all over the place to pet and ride the horses.

My husband had decided he needed more education. He was going on for his Masters in preaching. There was a Nazarene college in Nashville where he could get his Masters. He would have to go for three days at the beginning of the semester and three days at the end. The rest he could do on line from home or his office. It seemed he was always gone for something.

I had made friends with the librarian at the school where I worked. I helped her some in the library. She was a good Christian, and we talked about the Lord a lot; and she also loved horses. We began to talk about some girls we both had noticed who might need some special attention. These little girls were with single moms who were dating. My friend and I talked to the principal about a plan we had come up with. She said, "It should be fine." When my husband would be gone, we decided to invite these three girls over to my place, and we would have a girls spend-the-night. I would plan crafts for the girls to do or bake something with their help. They could play with each other, and Judy from the school library would come over and spend time with us too. Our place had a dead-end road that ran beside it, and Judy would help me lead the horses and give the girls rides on the horses each time they came. They loved taking the miniature horses out and playing with them and our dogs in the backyard.

One day I was out in the backyard doing chores, when a neighbor lady walked over to talk to me. I had not met her yet. She had a request. She had seen what we were doing with the girls and the horses. They had an eight-year-old granddaughter who suffered from seizures and was a brittle diabetic. Rebecca wore a pump to monitor her insulin at all times. They did not know how long they would have Rebecca with them. Rebecca had a dream that one day she would be able to ride a horse all by herself. Her grandmother asked if we would teach her to ride? I told her, "Yes, would be glad to work with her and help her learn to ride."

Rebecca was the sweetest little girl, and we grew to love her. Either her mother or grandmother came and stayed with us when she came to learn to ride, because Rebecca could not be left unattended night or day. We worked with her for some time teaching her to ride. By this time, we had acquired two more horses. The horse we decided might work best for Rebecca was a little Paso Fino, named Sin Par. She looked so cute on him and I know he knew he had a very special passenger on his back. Every time she rode that horse, he was perfect for her. I had ridden Paso Fino's for years. One thing I learned quickly about them was that they own you; you do not own them. It was easy to see right away, this little girl was Sin Par's. Rebecca had to stay close to her grandma or her mom, so it was mostly around our yard or little pasture where she would ride. It was her dream to go out for a trail ride. She wanted to ride her horse by herself. We saw how the horse was with Rebecca. God had His hand on both horse and rider. Rebecca came as often as she was able. We were in constant prayer for this little girl and in touch with her family. Rebecca seemed to have a little stretch of time when she did pretty well physically. We talked to her mom and grandma and they agreed to let us take Rebecca out on a trail ride. They agreed, but they would go and wait where we parked the truck and trailer in case Rebecca had a seizure. She could have a seizure without any apparent warning. We had a place only a few miles from where we lived that was for hikers and horses to use. We stayed on the two-track trails so that if her mom and grandmother needed to come and get her in the car they could drive on the wider trail. We often ran into the police using this park to train their tracking dogs also. This seemed a safe place to take Rebecca.

We loaded up the horses, and they followed us to the park. We were excited for Rebecca, and she was so excited. My husband, Rebecca, and I each had a horse; so, we put Rebecca between us, and off we went. I rode behind so I could constantly keep my eyes on Rebecca. Sin Par was so good with her. We rode about an hour. Rebecca finally had her dream come true. This Park had a little lake beside the trail, and we stopped to watch the geese swimming. It was a pretty little ride, and Rebecca was so happy. She finally got to ride a horse, by herself, on a trail ride.

Rebecca would come over to ride as often as she was able for as long as we lived there. We would have given her Sin Par, because her grandparents had the place for a horse. They said she could not have a horse because of her condition. She eventually got a special dog that could let them know when Rebecca was starting into a seizure.

If she was riding a horse, on a horse, she would be too far away from the dog, for the dog to be able to detect if she was going to have a seizure. This was a dream she had, and her family took the chance to see her dreamed fulfilled. We knew God was in this for her. We prayed and God worked.

Rebecca told her parents and grandparents it was okay, that she couldn't have a horse, because she had gotten to do what she had most wanted-to go on a trial ride. The Lord allowed us to be a part of making that little girl's dreams come true. I knew that having the farm and animals was in God's plans. He was using them for His purpose.

When I think back, my husband wanted to adopt a child when we were at our third church. Little did I realize; God had a much bigger plan in store for us. He had plans to bring a lot of children into our lives in a way I would have never dreamed of.

In this church, we had a teen leader Denise who loved the kids in her group and was very active with them. This church took part with the teens in all the activities the district had to offer. My husband and I went along to chaperone. We had a lot of teens, and several of us were needed to go to keep up with the kids. I would have devotion time with the girls that were in my room each night before we went to bed. It was a time of sharing a devotion, talking about what may be on their hearts, and praying with them. The girls seemed to look forward to this time each night. This helped me know them better and know how to pray for them. I would drive the church van to pick up kids when the regular driver could not make it. This helped me get a little closer to the kids also. Ever since our first church, I taught either an adult Sunday school class or a kid's class. I ended up teaching at about all levels over the years.

At this church I taught a children's class. When we lived in the subdivision, there was a little girl who lived there with a new baby brother and her parents. She got to know me, and the next thing I knew, when she could get out of the house, she would be peaking in my front door to see if she could see me anywhere in the house. If I was outside with the dogs, she would be right there with us. I would call her mom and tell her that her daughter was with me. Her parents did not think that people needed to go to church. "God loves everyone, and He saves everyone," was their thinking. Elizabeth wanted to go with us on to church, and they let her. She went with us Sunday mornings, and evening, and on Wednesday evenings. She was in my car going with me to any event she could attend. I prayed hard for that little girl because Satan was in her home to rob her of anything she was learning about God. She eventually gave her heart to Jesus. She was excited. When she got home and told her family she had given her heart to Jesus, her dad asked her "Why she did that," She told me, "Daddy says, 'Jesus saves everybody'." We prayed for that little girl.

I saw God working everywhere around me, but there were still problems in the home. You see, the big problem was me, so I was constantly told. (I remember being told that everything was my fault in my first marriage.) I did not believe that my husband ought to be able to travel with women alone, go out to lunch with a woman

alone, or counsel a woman alone when there was no one
else in the church. I was constantly told I was wrong,
and I was in the way of God using him to minister the
way he needed too. He left in the morning, and many
days I had no clue what he had done all day. He would
eat sometimes when he got home at night, and sometimes he would not. I never knew what to expect when
he walked in the door. All I knew was the Lord would
not let me leave him or do anything but wait upon the
Lord to do whatever it was in His will to do. *(I Samuel
26:9, But David said to Abishal, "Don't destroy him, for who
can lift a hand against the Lord's anointed and be innocent?"
CSB).* I had been shown through David's example with
Saul, I was not to touch God's anointed. I was to leave
the matter with the Lord. God would take care of it.

I had gotten acquainted with a lady who was the
prayer chaplain for a women's ministry. She traveled all
over the United States, and some other countries putting
on women's retreats. She lived not far from where we did,
and when she would be in town, she would call me to
meet her at the church and we would pray together at the
altar. Sometimes others in the area would be called to join
us if they could. I learned I could share with this woman,
and she would keep it to herself. I told her some of what
was going on in my life, and she would pray about it with
me. I told her how I felt about my husband going off with
women alone. She told me that I was right. She explained
to me that it could even make other people uncomfortable
to have them come to their house alone together. Many
people would know that it was not right for a pastor to

make calls with a woman other than his wife. She agreed to help me pray for my husband.

We stayed the longest at Louisville. I thought the Lord would leave us there for as long as He kept us in the ministry. It was eight hours home, and I had gotten to the point of trusting in the Lord to help me make the drive back to see family by myself. I knew the Lord was with me. My parents came and would spend a couple of weeks with us each summer. My kids came, and my husband's one brother and wife came quite often. I loved the women in my Bible study, the people in the church, and my work at the school with all the kids.

The church had built a new building with a larger sanctuary and more classrooms behind the existing church. This building got finished, and we were able to worship in the new building before my husband was wanting to leave again. The district office that was in the existing church when we arrived there, had built a house on the same property just across the parking lot and moved their offices in this place.

So, when the District Superintendent was in town, he was there at his office. One day he spoke to my husband and asked him what was going on at home. The people saw me upset one day. I did not know they realized there was anything wrong. I knew some of the people were treating my husband rather cool these days. When they saw me upset one morning, they finally took it to the D. S. My husband came home and exploded all over me. This was all my fault.

As I look back at a stack of journals I have here beside me, they are full of prayers I had been praying for both of us. I was still a new believer when I met my husband. I had heard some of his past and I was determined to be the best wife I could be. I loved my husband with all my heart. It took me a lot of years to realize I was putting him before God in my life. My husband consumed my mind and time, not God. I had to learn to put everything under God.

I had surrendered my life to God, but had a lot of cleaning out and learning to do about God's ways. The Lord had brought me into a circumstance in which He was going to let the refining fires burn hot for a lot of years, and He was going to hold me close to the flame to keep burning the dross off of me. The Lord had put the Devotional *Streams in the Desert* in my hands, and I was reading it over and over again. God began shedding light on what I was reading. In other words, I saw the words, but He wanted me to live what I was reading. From the first time I picked up *Streams in the Desert*, God 's plan was to make me more like Jesus, whatever it took. I had read that we are supposed to ask for Him to do this with us. I was praying this and He was answering my prayer. We could never guess into what circumstances the Lord will lead us to teach us to grow.

I loved my husband and wanted to be able to trust him and lean on him. After all, I had lost a man I dearly loved, and did lean on, and could trust. I thought that's what the Lord brought this person into my life for. I wanted to run from my husband's rejection, not him. I had a lot to learn yet about how God works. So, I guess my husband was right, it was all my fault.

18

ON THE MOVE AGAIN

My husband put his name out to other districts to find another church in which to minister. This time we would be moving five hours further away from family. We were moving straight South. I never wanted to live in the south. I prayed, begged and pleaded with the Lord not to make me go any further south. I was scared of snakes. The South has lots of poisonous snakes, and they get to be longer than I am tall. Fire ants, brown recluse spiders, scorpions, and black widow spiders are everywhere. I had read stories in *the National Geographic Magazine* if a cow in a field laid down by a big fire ant mound, the ants could kill a cow. The South may be pretty to visit, but please Lord, don't make me go live there. I knew the Lord would answer my prayer one way or another. It would be either "yes," "no" or in His time. He moved us south. I cried a lot, but God has His way. He is God.

We made the trip to interview. The church treasurer met us and took us to lunch and showed us around the church before we were to meet the church board and people. Warning flags came up in my heart. There was something unsettling about the church treasurer. I knew deep down in the pit of my stomach that in this place my marriage was not going to get any better.

We were voted in at the church. Next, we had to find a place to live. We looked with a realtor for a whole day, and we found nothing. We went back to Louisville, and I started looking for a small farm on the internet, praying that the Lord would help us find a place. My daughter was also looking on the internet to see if she could help us find a place in Russellville, Alabama. I finally ran across a small farm about eight miles from the church, but the place was run down and needed a lot of work. I did not like the house. There was no storage; the laundry room had been put in the garage making it impossible to park a car there. The outside needed painting, and every window was broken with duct tape holding the broken pieces in place. The list was long of remodeling and repairs that needed to be done. I showed it to my daughter and she said, "Mom, look at the land; The house can be fixed, but look at the land, it is beautiful." The place did have a dog kennel, barn and tractor shed. The dog kennel would help when we would have to be gone over night. The dogs could go in and out into a fenced-in yard as they wanted too. Maybe we could find someone we could pay to come in and take care of all the animals a couple of times a day.

We made a day trip there to look at the property. We met the realtor at the farm, but the lady who was living in the house was home also. She was an older lady, and her husband had died of a heart attack seven years before. She was trying to stay on living in this place by herself, but her health was failing her. She and her husband had raised their children there. They had cattle, horses and sheep. She raised and trained sheep-herding dogs for years. This lady and her daughter would compete in one-hundred-mile endurance rides on their horses. She had a whole life worth of memories tied up in this place. She did not want to move. Her children were making her move, because her health was failing, and because they didn't live near her. Barbara's kids had gotten her five aces in another community about twenty-five-miles from this place. It was just down the road from her daughters, and they built a place for her to move to and a place for the sheep she still had left. Barbara said it was nice, but she did not want to leave her place.

When I saw all that needed to be done to the house up close, it became even more overwhelming. Every roof needed replacing. Where there had been a covered porch on the back of the house, it had been closed in to make another room. The windows had leaked so badly that a person could poke his finger through the wood by the windows. Two whole walls in this room had to be replaced. I felt the Lord speak to me and I agreed to take the place. I was learning to do, what I knew He was telling me to do, no matter what.

Doug, one of the men in the church, had told us about a bank in town where we may be able to get financing.

He said he knew the President of the bank, and he would take us there to meet him and see about financing the farm. We called Doug, and he called and set up a time for us to meet the bank president. When we went in to meet the bank President, it crossed my mind to ask him if there were any job openings at the bank. I told him that we would be moving here in a couple of months, and I would be looking for a job. He told me to check back with him when we got moved here. He owned a lot of businesses in the area, and if the bank did not have an opening, he would see what might be available at one of his other places. So we went back to Louisville for my husband to resign his position at the church, start packing again.

This time we had our five dogs, a scarlet macaw parrot, sugar glider and six horses to move, as well as, a small tractor we did not have before when we moved. The realtor helped us find people to do the repairs that we could not do and that needed to be done before we moved in. It was about a month before we came back again with our first load. We had bought a bed from the lady who had owned the house. So, when we made this first trip back, we knew we had a place to sleep. All I had to do was bring bedding to make the bed. We got the pastures ready to bring three horses the next trip. The next trip we both drove and left the car here with the horses. There was plenty of grazing for them and a pond for all the water they needed. We would be back in a couple of days with the final load and the rest of the horses and dogs, a scarlet macaw parrot and sugar glider.

When we got to the farm the first time, I went out to check the fence line to make sure it was sound enough to hold the horses. I was coming along the fence and the grass was pretty tall. I had on jeans, socks, and tennis shoes. I could not believe it. I stepped into a huge fire ant hill. They were all over me in a heartbeat. They were inside my jeans biting me like crazy. I got out of my jeans and headed to the house as fast as I could go. My legs were on fire. I knew that when a mosquito bites me, the swelling would last for a few days. What I feared, happened. I swelled up more with fire ant bites that can last a week or two. I tried everything the drug store had to offer. Nothing worked to relieve the swelling and burning itch.

We went back to Louisville for the last big haul. There was a guy, named Bruce from the Louisville church who agreed to drive another U-Haul, because this time I would be hauling horses, and my husband would be diving a U-Haul. We needed two U-Hauls to get everything moved. So off we went: two U-hauls towing trailers loaded with a tractor, a lawn mower and other possessions. I was driving our truck pulling a 30′ horse trailer loaded up with all the remaining horses and animals. We barely got out on the expressway and were getting up to speed, when a person in the left-hand lane cut right between my husband and Bruce, the guy driving the other U-Haul. I was behind Bruce. Bruce hit his brakes; I hit mine. I thought for sure Bruce was going to hit this person. We still do not know how there was not a wreck. It had to have been the Lord's hand protecting us, is all I know. I realized right away something was wrong within the horse trailer. We stopped as soon as we could get off the highway to check things out. My husband saw what had happened behind him. Sure enough, there was something wrong with Mofiosa, the horse that was loaded last in the trailer. Both of her back legs had gone up under her, and she was sitting on the floor with her back legs straight out in front of her. The way she was, she could not get back on her feet by herself. It took the three of us to get her on her feet. The Lord had to be with her, for she was fine when we got her back on her feet, and she rode the rest of the way calm and quiet. The other two horses were fine also. I was praising the Lord for what He was doing.

After this incident everything was going well until we got about three hours into the trip, and we ran into the worst thunder and lightning storm. Rain was coming down so hard we could barely see in front of us, and cloud to ground lightening was like I do not think I had ever seen before. I was praying and telling the Lord I did not want to be doing this anyway, asking Him, "What is going on?" I know He controls every lightning bolt, the wind and rain. He did keep us safe through the storm. I was praising Him for that. We pulled into the farm much later than we had planned. We were exhausted by the time we finally got the animals settled in so we could eat something and go to bed. On the first trip before we had made bringing the first three horses to the farm, we had brought a spare bed, so we had a place ready for Bruce to sleep that night.

If this difficulty was happening just to get here, what was coming for the future? about those refining fires the Lord uses Remember my previous mention of those refining fires the Lord uses to make us look more like Him? He was going to turn the heat up to red hot under me.

We had moved in just before Thanksgiving. I had no kitchen; it was torn up. I was getting a totally new kitchen. There were boxes stacked to the ceiling in the garage and furniture was stacked to the ceiling in the living room or in the middle of other rooms. I had about thirty gallons of paint to put on walls and ceilings. Thanksgiving Day one of the church members brought over a turkey dinner for us from Walmart. We were so grateful. I had nothing to cook on. Mr. and Mrs. Prince, neighbors who live at the end of the dead-end road we live on, brought in a home-made pie and introduced themselves to us.

When I could find our clothes and my kitchen was put in, I called the bank to tell them I was in town and to see if they had a job opening. I was told that they had a job opening, but it would not be available until January sometime. The people in the church knew I needed a job, so they were keeping their eyes open for me. There was a guy who worked at a large car lot, and an opening was coming up for a person to keep inventory of all the cars coming in and going out. I went in to apply for the job. It sounded interesting. I interviewed, and the lady wanted to hire me. She was a believer, and when she found out I was also, she really wanted me to work there. A lot of the people there were believers. A couple of days after I interviewed, I got a call from her telling me that the young lady I was supposed to replace that she was keeping her job. The Lord shut the door on that job. Someone told me about an opening in an auto glass repair shop. The owners were looking for someone to work in the office. I went there to check it out. The guy had just hired someone the day before. I thought maybe of going to apply at the school to get a job back in the school system. A person gave me an application, told me to take it home, to fill it out and bring it back. When I took it back, it was the wrong application. She gave me another one. When I filled it out and went back, the person who did the interviewing was on vacation for a couple of weeks. I decided that maybe I was supposed to go to work for the bank, and I waited for them to call me. I had about finished my painting and getting settled in. My brother-in-law and sister-in-law came at Christmas to help us get furniture moved into place after we had painted. My husband's brother put up several mercury lights to enable us to see what might be underfoot when we had to be outside at night with the animals. They lived in Michigan but loved to travel. We were so grateful for all their help.

I finally got the call from the bank and started working January 28, 2008. I was going to be working in a new department that was being created-the imaging department. Every document that passes through the bank of any kind has to be imaged, and the information stored for several years. I had worked at a bank before my children were born. I worked at a bank for five years up to a week before having my first baby, Melissa, in my home town Midland, Michigan. I liked the work that I did at the bank.

My husband was still taking classes for his master's degree. We were the same distance from Nashville as we were when we lived in Louisville, Ky. It was not long after Christmas when he was back in class. He would have to go and attend class at the beginning of the term for a few days, come home and work online, then he would have to go back at the end of the class.

I started my new job. There were a lot of people packed in one place with all different personalities. I was walking into a new kind of stress. I do not know how to describe it, but I came home crying a lot of days. I knew God had put me there, and I knew I was not to leave until He released me. I did love the work that I did.

The more the Lord used me with some people, the more Satan used others to come at me. I met some young people there who left the bank before me to go on to other places and jobs with whom I am still friends. While they sat beside me working, I was able to share with them about the Lord. I can see now that the Lord was using the pounding, I took there to get me into the shape He wanted me to be in. I said I used to hate. I began to realize that Satan was trying to lead me into that old bondage again. Thank goodness the Lord let me see what was happening and was showing me constantly what Jesus did for us on the cross. I was constantly reminded of this: you do not have to like the sin, but pray for the sinner. The Lord put me there, to not only test me, but to really work it out in my heart to pray for others. I will admit, I didn't hate them, but it did take some time before I could pray for them. It hurts when people turn on you, and you don't know why. I had to learn to deal with the hurt first, before I could really pray for those who hurt me. Some of my co-workers needed someone who could pray for them. Satan knew this, so he tried to inspire the people who needed the prayer, to hurt those who could pray for them. Satan tried to stop any prayer going up for these people. God works when His children pray, and

Satan will do anything he can to stop those prayers from being prayed.

This process was going to take some time. I am still a work in progress. Meantime at home, there was a man from the church, who at one time raised and showed horses. He had made money raising and showing Tennessee Walker horses. He thought if he could get my husband and me interested this was going to be his big opportunity to get into raising and showing horses again. I did not feel this was the direction the Lord wanted my husband and me to go. But my husband ignored me because he wanted to do this. I had learned my lesson with the miniature horses and did not feel that this was what the Lord wanted us to do.

While I was at work, the two of them would go off and look at horses without telling me what they were going to do. When I came home from work there would be another horse. I was told to write the other guy a check for our half of the price of the horse. In other words, I was to do chores and write checks, otherwise, I was to keep quiet. I prayed for God to help me. I kept getting, "I will walk through the trial with you. Just be still and know I am God." It is one thing to read about it, and another to go through the fire. God is there with us, but no matter what way you look at it, when the fire is burning, and you are standing close, it hurts.

One day when this guy was here talking to my husband, they did not see me walking up behind them. I caught my husband telling this guy, "I have to keep her here. I can't do all this by myself." We were up to twenty some horses on the place. We had pregnant mares due to foal. They were going to make money off goats selling them for meat. We had acquired many goats and a donkey to protect the goats from the coyotes.

It was not long before this guy and my husband were at odds with each other, and their big plans started falling apart. I started getting hard feelings toward this guy, but in time, the Lord checked me and made me repent. The Lord let me see this guy for what he was not to get mad at him, but to pray for him. It took a little time, but the Lord finally softened my heart, so that I really could pray for this man. The Lord softened my heart, and I would send him some homemade baked goods once in a while. He was really old and his wife had died a few months before all these plans for the horses manifested with us. This man pushed hard for us to come to this church. When he found out we had horses, he was in constant contact with my husband before we even got here. I think he saw us as his dream coming alive again. The Lord saw to it that Rebecca's the little girl from Louisville, dream was going to be fulfilled. This guy's dreams were to become smashed to pieces. When we finally get through the trial, it is amazing to look back and trace the hand of the Lord, and how He works out all life's circumstances for His purposes.

I married my husband because I loved him; he had no money. I began to realize his motive for marrying me was because I had some. I told him one day that with the fall of the stock market a few years before, and the way the money was going out the door, what I had left was not going to last too much longer.

People who worked at the bank with me and from the church started telling me they were seeing this lady, who had taken us out to dinner the first day we came to interview, at the church and my husband out a lot together. This was the lady who caused the red flags to come in my heart. This could be the one that might pull him away. People were seeing them out eating together; they were making hospital calls together. I faced him with it, but he told me it was church business. My husband had always said, "If you tell a lie long enough everyone will believe it." That was not going to work here. He was the only one believing his own lies, if anyone was believing them. As a matter of fact, no one was.

He came home from his last class that he needed to take for his Master's degree in preaching and informed me that he had stopped in on his way home at a truck driving school to sign up to learn to become an over the road truck driver. He was leaving the ministry. He resigned from the church and went to truck driving school. He was able to drive back and forth from the house each day. He was assigned a truck to drive, and there was another guy, besides the instructor, who was learning to drive in the same truck with him. They had to take turns driving each day. This young man's family lived out of state, and we had him over on the weekends. He was to share with me later that my husband's lady friend would be on the phone to him all the time.

I did not know my husband was really planning on leaving me. The Lord had held me with him. I thought the Lord would surely open my husband's eyes to see what He would be doing to God and the church if he kept on the path he was going down. When he finished the truck driving school, he was going to have to go out on the road for six weeks. This meant I was going to be alone for six weeks. I called and invited his mother to come and stay with me for the six weeks. She lived alone in Michigan. I had gone and stayed at his mother's when we lived in Illinois near them and took care of her husband when she was in the hospital. When I was off from working in the school system during the summer months, I would go help them whenever they needed help. They lived a couple of hours away from us in Southern Illinois. His mom came and stayed with me. She had planned on staying the whole six weeks with me. He got mad at me for asking her to come. I did not understand why this would make him mad at the time.

I liked his mom and we had a good time together. She liked our devotion time together every morning. She knew what time I got up to start my day in devotions and prayer. When I got up, she would be sitting at the dining room table waiting for me to get there. We had Bible reading and I would read a section from *Oswald Chambers Complete Works*. Last, we would pray. We never missed a morning. On weekends, I would take her different places to see the pretty country down here. She had never been in Alabama before.

His mom came in the night before I had to take my husband to the bus stop to go to Atlanta, Georgia. After truck driving school, the student has to work for a company who has trainers with whom they have to drive for six weeks. His mom went with me to put him on the bus to head for the company he would be working for. I never said anything to his mother about what I knew was going on between her son and this other lady. My husband was gone a few weeks, and I came home from work one night and got a call from him, "I have been put off the truck. I am back in Atlanta, Georgia. You come get me tonight. If you don't come, I will get someone else to come get me." I knew who that someone would be. He had been put off the truck because he forgot about a traffic ticket, he had gotten several years ago. They found out about it and put him off the truck the first chance they got.

His mom could hear him talk to me and she said, "Let's go get him." She had no clue who that someone else would be who would go get him. I did chores, and we headed out for a ten-hour round trip. They would have paid for him a bus ticket the next day and put him up for the night, but he wasn't waiting. His mom and I got in the truck and went. We got back the next morning, and I had one hour of sleep until I had to go back to work for the day.

He and his mom spent the day together. He must have told her he was leaving me, because the very next morning, as soon as we got up, she was packed and heading out the door to go home. She would not stay.

He had not told me yet that he was actually leaving me, except he kept saying, "I hear that after paying $250.00 and waiting 30 days, if there are no kids, a divorce is final here in Alabama." He was looking for another trucking job, but also was seeing a lawyer about a divorce. I did not know he had filed for divorce until he had another job. Just before he was supposed to be leaving, he told me he was going to pick me up from work at lunch one day for me to go sign the divorce papers. That's how I found out he had filed. I was trying to tell him this was not right, and the Lord hates divorce. He was a pastor; he should know better. He said, "No, I am not any longer a pastor. I quit the church. I am not a pastor anymore." He had it all planned out. He took me in the lawyer's office and went to the secretary's desk and got the papers I needed to sign. I cried, and told him again that this was wrong. He stood over me and said, "Vicki, you sign those papers." I did. The secretary told him they would submit the papers when he got the rest of the money. I did not know for sure where he was going to get the money; he was not working and had no money coming in, but I should have guessed.

A couple of days after this, I drove home from work one night to see a "For Sale" sign in front of the farm. When I got in and had parked, there he was repainting the little building the goats stayed in. He wanted this place sold fast. He was demanding money from me. He put the farm up for sale because he wanted money when it sold. He had said nothing to me, and had gone on his own and gotten a realtor and put the place up for sale. He had gotten the money for the divorce, but said nothing to me indicating he had gotten the money. He stayed at the house until the day before I was to take him to the bus to head for another trucking job. I went to the mailbox, and there were the final papers. It was all over. He thought I would not get the papers until after he left. The lawyers had told my husband that the courts were backed up and it might take a little longer than usual to get the divorce finalized.

This woman, who was just a friend, is now his wife. In time this district let him back in the ministry, and I really pray God will get ahold of both of them one day. I can really pray for them. They thought they had been clever and had deceived God. If they only realized they were deceiving themselves, not God. If they do not get it right, when they meet Jesus, it is not going to be good.

The news of what happened traveled back to every church where we had ministered. I don't know how word travels, but it does. People from our last churches started calling me to see if I was alright. I found out why we had to keep moving. They did not like some of the things they saw him doing after we had been in their churches for a while. I thought it was my fault, and the people were mad at me for some reason. Some of them keep track of me to this day.

The night the final divorce papers came through, my husband was still staying at the house with me. He had expected to be gone the next day, and he had been told I would get the papers the following week, after he was gone. When the papers came, he took off and came back later that night.

After he left that evening, I was in my backyard with the papers in my hands crying and pacing back and forth. I was shouting at God and holding the papers up in the air, "Why, Father? Why did you bring him into my life? It was fifteen years wasted. "I got an answer right back. I was pretty distraught, and this time the Lord did not speak in a whisper, but loudly. I heard, "I was after Abraham, not Isaac." I knew what God meant. As God tested Abraham to see if he would be obedient and offer his only son as a sacrifice to God, God was using this situation to test my obedience to Him. He was using this to grow me spiritually.

God was really after me, and He used this guy to get me where He wanted me. I had to go sit down in awe of God. He spoke again to me, and what He said. I would never have dreamed; He was after me. He had said He wanted my husband back in the ministry, but God does not give details, He lets us live the details out. Then we know, that we know about what He is up to. He wanted my husband back, because he was going to use my husband and all the circumstances around his life to work on me. Who would think? But I was learning. God does not think the way we do. His thoughts are so much higher than ours. I knew I had to grow, but we never dream how God is going to give us the opportunity to work that out.

I called my kids to tell them that I had gotten the divorce papers. I told them I was pacing back and forth across the back yard and shouting at God when He spoke to me and what He said. They were not sad. They did not like the way I was being treated. Rod told me, "Just let me know when, and I will be down there to bring you home, Mom." Missy and Marc had two children, and they were all excited that I would be coming home again. But, again, that was our plan, not God's.

The next morning at 4:00 a.m. my phone rang. My kids knew I was usually up about that time to be with the Lord. It was Missy, my daughter. "Mom," she said, "are you up? I couldn't wait to call you. You know how you tell me God talks to you. Well, He woke me up at midnight to tell me, to tell you, 'It was not fifteen years wasted; it was fifteen years that made you grow.'" She said, "I am not sure which I am most excited about, what He told me, or the fact I heard Him, just like you said you hear Him." I could not believe it, God had finally spoken to one of my children. Missy was so excited; she had not been able to sleep waiting for the time to pass so that she could call me.

19

WHAT ARE YOU GOING TO DO NOW?

J knew God was with me, and He would lead me, so I got down on the floor and asked Him, "What are You going to do now?" Have you ever heard that song, "If I ever needed the Lord, I sure do need Him now?" He had cleaned any independence in myself out of me. I didn't have a clue what to do. I knew God was sovereign; He was with me; He was still talking to me, and He had the plan. I told Him; He was going to have to take care of me; I did not know what to do.

The pressure was off one way at home, but a new one started. Work was no better. I wrote scripture and sayings on note cards and had them all over my desk at work. On one card I had written, "Just trust God for His sake, not mine or anyone else's. No matter what I think I see, just trust God. Like Abraham & Isaac, if You take me to it, You will take me through it. Yield-Trust-Obey." I had these scripture and notes written on bright colored note cards. The colors cheered me, and the words held me. At home I had Bibles and books all over that I could pick up to get my mind focused on the Lord when my situation started getting more than I thought I could handle. I was learning to lean on God. He had me where He wanted me. All my family lived fourteen hours away. I was all alone, just Jesus and me. All I had was God, and, in time, I was going to learn He was all I needed.

There was no point for me to stay here by myself that I could see. I started planning on moving back home, so a good place to start was getting rid of stuff. I could not handle all the animals and could not afford to keep them up the way they needed to be kept anyway. The neighbor man helped me load up the goats in his stock trailer, and he hauled them to the stock yard to sell for me. I called the man who was in the deal with the horses and let him know what had happened. He took several horses off the place. I had a donkey that was running with the goats to protect the goats from the coyotes. I gave away the donkey and some of the horses and sold some of them. I ended up selling the horses at a fraction of what was paid for them. It upsets me when I see people have animals and not take care of them like they should be cared for. My main concern was getting these horses where they would get good care.

A few months after I was alone, I had gotten a call from some women who had been in my Bible study in Louisville, Ky. They had found out that I was alone and they wanted to come and spend a few days with me. I really missed this group of ladies. I would be thrilled to have them. I had room for the ones who could come to stay at my house. I was so excited I could hardly stand it. I was planning some of the meals, for us and we had planned on traveling around some each day they were here. I started praying for the Lord to plan our days for us.

Finally, the day came when they arrived. God had it all planned out for us. I had not planned anything but a devotional for us all to share. The devotional would be what I was already reading myself each morning and prayer, and then we would be off sight-seeing for the day.

The first morning we all felt His presence with us. We were reading, praying, sharing all morning until lunch. The Lord would lead me to read whatever He wanted me to share besides the devotional. I am a reader and have a small library of spiritual books. I was led to the book and section He wanted read. It would always be something someone needed to hear. A lot of praying, sharing and healing went on. Hearts shared things that had been bottled up for a long time. It ended up being a women's retreat on a small scale. We would eat lunch out somewhere, tour around and come back for the evening. The evenings went the same as the mornings until we dropped into bed. I needed this and so did they.

The next year the same ladies came back again, and the Lord came in our midst again. This time they flew in and rented a car and drove to my home. We had decided that the day before they had to leave, I would follow them back to Birmingham and we would stay in a motel and explore Birmingham, for a day. We had the best time, and I was praising the Lord again; it was a time we all needed.

I had stopped going to the church where we had been ministering. Under the circumstances, it was best if I left the church. The Lord finally led me to a church not far from my home, Calvary Baptist Church. I had tried another church first but did not feel the Lord was wanting me to be there. I made a couple of friends at Calvary right away. One lady had just lost her husband to cancer. So, we started doing things together. She was keeping an eye on her mom who was not well, but still able to get out. Lots of times she would go with Judy and me, out to dinner or shopping.

By this time, I had two horses left. You see when you give yourself to the Lord completely, He will empty us of everything that would come before Him. I mean everything; He does not miss a thing. Horses and animals had been my passion since I could remember. I realize I had put my husband before the Lord; he was gone. Now the Lord was putting me to the test with the horses. He allowed me to get exhausted and drained down to the last drop. It was a real rainy fall. This farm is built on clay soil on a huge rock. I was having to wade through the clay to take care of all those horses and animals. I was having to carry hay by the arm loads out and make twenty some piles. They were strung out all over the back pasture so each horse had its own pile of hay. It would be pouring rain, and I had muck boots on that came to my knees, but I would sink so deep in the mud when I walked, I would end up out of them. What a mess.

There were two tractors here when my husband left. One could handle round bales, but I could not afford to make payments on it any longer. There was also something wrong with it. I could operate the equipment, but I am not a mechanic. Not long after I was alone, my septic tank gave me problems, and it had to be replaced. Not much longer after this, my furnace had to be replaced. I was moving anyway, so I sold both tractors to get rid of a payment and pay for the two things I needed to replace. So, I had no tractor to move those big round bales. I was using square bales, and I had to wade mud twice a day to feed livestock. Two mares were due to have babies. I was able to help the one foal be born, but it was deformed, and it did not live long. The other mare's baby was born with its ears presenting first, upside down with its feet toward its mothers' spine. When I examined her and could feel that the baby was coming the wrong way, I rushed in and called the vet. He got right out here. The baby had to be taken from the mother in such a way it did not live. I had seen this happen with one of my miniature horses. It tears me up. I told the Lord, "Help me get these horses into good homes, and I will not ask you for anymore horses. I don't want them anymore."

He had answered my prayer down to the last two horses. My friend Judy and I were at the movies watching "Tangled;" I was intently watching one of the characters and his horse interacting with each other. It was a beautiful white horse. The Lord spoke to me again. He said, "It is time to love your horses again." I remember in my mind, telling God, "I don't want them anymore." He came back at me, "It's not about you."

When I got home that night I went to the barn and turned on the light and went in with Falina and Red, the two Tennessee Walking horses I had left, and I could feel a love come into my heart again for them. But I had learned, they would never be put before God.

I was going to be tested in another way. I loved dogs; I had several, but one in particular never lets me out of his site. He is a little guy, and shortly after this with the horses, the Lord woke me one morning with this message, "I want you to give Joshua away." By now I was going to do whatever the Lord said, no matter how much it hurt. One of the neighbors had been telling me about another lady who lived further down the road who was retiring from work, and she and her husband wanted a little dog. I called my friend and asked her if they might want Joshua. She talked to the lady, and told me that they would take the dog. This was on a weekend when Joshua went to live with this couple. I was hearing how they took Joshua to be all groomed and bought him all kinds of toys, and Joshua would sit next to her husband all the time. I knew he had gone to a good home. I missed him, but I told myself, "This is what the Lord wants, get over it." I could have gone to see him, but that would not be fair to Joshua. Joshua would not understand why he could not come home with me. I made up my mind to let him go.

The next Sunday morning, about the time I was getting up for my devotions, just as I was waking up, the Lord spoke to me again. "Joshua will be back before church tonight." I thought, "No, this couldn't be. They loved Joshua." It was about 4:00 p.m., before church that evening; I got a call for the lady who had Joshua telling me, "You have to take Joshua back. Joshua won't eat anything for us. We have tried everything. He won't eat." I told her to bring him back. She put him in the car and brought him right back. Joshua was home before church that night, just like the Lord had told me that morning. When the lady put Joshua back into my arms, I had to apologize to her. I told her the Lord had used her to test me. Would I be obedient? I explained to her what was going on. I offered to pay her for any money she had put into Joshua that week. She is a good Christian and was so excited that the Lord had used her. She told me I was not to pay her back. Their children had dogs, and they were going to give the toys they got for Joshua to their dogs. My little Joshua was back and is still following me everywhere. It doesn't matter if it's to the barn, a walk in the fields or in the house, he is going to be with me, if he can. As a matter of fact, he is lying in his little basket beside me now as I write this book.

Just about this time, the Lord was about to give me something to rejoice in. My son had not married yet and was not dating. When mom passed, he was alone living in the Detroit area where he worked. He was active in church and had lots of friends who did things together, but there was no one special in his life. He met a young lady who had never been married at church when she and her mom started going there. Rod and Alison started dating. Rod and I talked a lot, and it helped to have him to talk to. In time, he called me and told me he wanted to ask Alison to marry him, but before he did, he wanted me to meet her. I had not been able to get to Michigan for some time after the divorce with all I had going on here at the farm. I was down to two horses and my dogs by this time.

He said they would fly in, and I could pick them up at the airport, and if I did not mind sharing a bed with

Alison, he would take us to Atlanta, Georgia to tour around for a couple of days. We would then come back to the farm for a couple of days so that Alison could see it. He had not told Alison anything, other than to ask if she wanted to go to Alabama to meet me and then go to Atlanta, Georgia to sightsee. Alison had a sister who lived in the Carolinas. Alison and Jen made arrangements for Jen to drive over to meet us in Atlanta for a day. God is so good. Just when a person is at the bottom, God brings something to lift us back up. I was so excited for my son.

Six months had gone by, and it was time to renew the listing on the farm with the realtor, or change realtors. The farm had not been shown at all. I had gotten a new supervisor at work, and he told me of a local Christian realtor. He said that she was really good. He told me where she was, and I went to see her. I liked her right away. So, I signed up for her to list the farm.

They had the house listed for about six months. They were showing it and had lots of responses on the farm. They all fell apart before anyone could buy it. She would send me a report of how many showings and inquiries each month they had. I saw the advertising, and I know they were getting the farm out there for the people to see. Then one morning, again, as I was waking, the Lord came and spoke to me, "I want you to take the farm off the market." I responded, "But Father this company has put so much money into advertising, and my ex-husband is demanding money from the sale of the farm. I have sold the tractors; I am half packed and ready to go. Besides, Lord, this is Saturday morning, there may not be anyone in the reality office today." I got out of bed and journaled what He had told me to do and opened one of my devotionals and read, "If the Lord tells you to do something, do not tarry. Do it now." I heard Him. I got chores done, got my shower and got ready to go. I was at the realtor's office door at 8:00 a.m.

I walked up to the door, and I could see someone in the back. I tried the door and it was open. The owner, who had listed the place, was there. I walked in, and she came to greet me. I started to say, "You will never guess why I am here." She said, "You are here to take the place off the market." I stared at her in disbelief. She said, "We have all been wondering how long it was going to take you to listen to the Lord. You are not going anywhere." There was a chair beside me and I sank in it. She kept talking, "The Lord is not going to let us sell that place, and we have been taking bets around this office as to how long it's going to take you to listen to the Lord. When any of us go out to your place to show it or check on things, we can feel a presence so strong there. We know Who it is." I did not have to tell her anything. She told me. She gave me a hug and sent me on my way.

20

STAYING, NOW WHAT?

This opened a whole new set of circumstances that I had not begun to consider. I would have to come up with the money to pay my ex-husband off and to pay bills, I did not know how I was going to be able to handle this. My supervisor kept telling me at work that I couldn't go anywhere. I told him about what happened when I went to the realtor on Saturday. He suggested I go talk to a loan officer in the bank. So, I went to the one who had written up the loan on the farm. I shared with him my situation. Right away he told me that the mortgage rates had dropped drastically. To reduce the mortgage, he advised me to search out different insurance companies to see who might offer less expensive coverage. Another person I worked with shared with me where her family got insurance. I could not believe the drop in cost for the same coverage for the truck and home. The Lord had it all planned out; I just had to get with the program. When I followed the trail, the Lord led me on,

I was going to be alright. I was in awe of how my God works. He never ceases to amaze me.

I still had a problem. I had forty acres in the South. The woods and fields can get so dense with brush and vines, that it can get almost to the point that a person cannot walk through it. This was not a problem I had dealt with when I lived in the North. Poison ivy grows about four or five inches high in the North. Here it can over take a tree. I had sold my tractor and brush hog; how was I going to keep this place cleared out? Two horses could not eat that much. It was getting so that some of the weeds where higher than the horses. I was talking with the neighbor man who had cattle on his place. He said, "Why don't you lease your land to someone to bring in cattle to help keep it cleared?" He said, "I know someone looking for about the area you have here." The property was divided off in several sections so the cattle could be separate from my horses. He sent the guy over to talk to me. We worked it out and he brought in some cattle. What a big help. I praised the Lord; another situation had been solved. The Lord was opening the way.

My son had gotten engaged to Alison, and a year later they were getting married. I was getting to go home for the wedding. I had a different supervisor at work. When she learned my son was getting married, she and her husband decided she would take me shopping and get me the dress I could wear at my son's and Alison's wedding. A neighbor came in and took care of the animals for me, and my supervisor drove me to the airport and picked me up when I flew back. The Lord was providing for me and had the right people in my life at the right time.

That next winter, I was coming out of the back door in the morning to do chores. The deck was old and slippery. There was black ice on it and I did not see it. I got a few steps out, and my feet went straight out from under me. I came straight down on my spine. I sat there for the longest time but could not move because the pain was so intense. I felt sick to my stomach. I don't know how long I sat there. Finally, I was able to make it up. I went on to do chores and get ready to go to work. I did not go to the doctor; I did not have good insurance, and I could not afford to be laid up. I did find out later I had fractured a couple of vertebrae in my back.

I had been alone down here in the South for about two and a half years living by myself. I had a huge oak tree that was looking like it could go down any minute. It was leaning toward the barn with fencing on two sides of it. I remembered that there was a man at the church, his name was James. There was a man in the church, where we used to minister, who had a fireplace and loved to cut hard wood to use in it. He had been married to a friend's sister. I had my friend call James to see if he would want to look at the tree. He could have the wood if he wanted to come cut it down. He came to look at it, but it was too close to the barn, and too big. James did not think he could handle a tree that size by himself and keep it from landing on the barn.

A few days later we had a big storm with lots of rain and wind during the night. When I got up in the morning, I could not believe what I saw. That huge tree was lying on the ground in the only way it could have gone down to cause the least damage. It was laid down between two fence posts in a pasture opposite the barn. It was like the hand of God laid that tree down. It only broke the four boards that were between the two posts on the north side of the tree. I called my friend and told her to call James and tell him he could come get the tree; the Lord laid it on the ground for him last night.

The next morning, James was there with his truck and trailer before I went to work to start cutting the tree up. He could hardly believe what he saw. He started working on it. It was going to take a few days to cut up the huge oak tree that the Lord look down for us and lay sprawled out across the pasture. He came every day and finally got everything cleaned up for me. I was grateful that the tree was gone. James wanted the hard wood to burn.

James' wife had died of cancer about a year before this time, and he was alone. I knew James and his wife a little, as they attended the Nazarene church where we were ministering before my husband left me. James lived in another little town about twenty miles from the church and passed the road I lived on. He said he heard the Lord speak to him as he was leaving the church the next Sunday, "Call her." He had my home phone number. I was not home from church yet, so I did not answer. He got almost to my road, and he said, he heard, "Try again." This time I answered. He asked if he could come by and talk for a few minutes. I said that would be fine.

After all that had happened in my life, I had made up my mind that I was not going to have anyone in my life again. I was in my 60's, and I did not need any more men in my life. I was fine the way I was. I could put my full attention on the Lord. After all, I figured that's what would please Him.

James had not been in the house before. He did not know about my Scarlet Macaw parrot. I kept all the dogs in the house or dog kennel when he was cutting down the tree, so they would not be in his way. He did not know that if someone walks in the door, and Red, my parrot, decides he does not like the person, my parrot will scream so loudly it will about deafen a person. The bird is in a room I call my bird room. When people come in the back door they enter into this room. Red greets about everyone who enters the house. Red can talk and tells people he knows and likes, "Hello," when they come in. There is a big archway going into the living room. I put James on the couch where Red could see him. The little dogs were loose in the house. I sat in a chair across from James where Red did not see me. Red made no sound. He was absolutely quiet the whole time James was here. Red will usually do things to try to attract attention if he likes people. Not that day. I thought that Red must like James and was just listening to him talk.

My little dogs like people, and I did not stop them from being all over James. I thought we would see how he did with the dogs. I could tell he kept talking and playing with the dogs. He was enjoying the dogs. As he talked on, I was to find out he had two little dogs in his house and three big dogs in his fenced in backyard. I had four little dogs inside and two big dogs outside. I found out that James liked dogs.

James started talking and telling me a little about himself. He was married to a lady for thirty-nine years.

She had passed from being disabled with rheumatoid arthritis most of their married life. They were not able to have children. He and his wife, who had passed a year ago, had been married three years when she passed with cancer. He liked to go to gospel music concerts, and it would be nice to have someone to go with him. Well, I liked to go to them too. After talking for a while, we did seem to have a lot in common. I guess it would be okay to have a friend.

James and I had begun spending time together for about a year. I had a pastor friend back in Louisville, Kentucky, who was up in years and very sickly. His wife was a friend of mine when I lived there. They would call and check on me every now and then to see how I was doing. He had been in and out of the hospital on the brink of death. He had started a church in Shepherdsville, Kentucky, just south of Louisville and had been the pastor there for forty years. I got a call from Robert, asking me to pray for him. In a few weeks the church was going to have a forty-year celebration for him. He wanted me to pray the Lord would let him live long enough to make it to his 40th anniversary with this church. They wanted to know if I could make it that weekend for the event. It was going to be a Saturday evening and Sunday morning celebration. James knew how to take care of all the animals by now, and he told me to go; he would take care of the farm. Robert lived to make it to his celebration. He had called me on my cell phone to make sure I was making it alright when I was on my way from Alabama to Shepherdsville. It was a five-hour trip one way. Those two people had the biggest heart for people. They loved people, and people loved them.

I saw a lot of pastors and wives, and people I had not seen since we left the district. Pat and Eugene, the lady who was so excited in my Bible study to have a pastor's wife of her own, had made the trip from Georgia where they had moved. We talked for a long time, and I was telling them about James. I told them he was a wonderful man, but I did not want any permanent relationship with a man again. Being friends was fine, but I didn't want anything more. Eugene started to talk to me about the Lord. We all knew that the Lord had brought James into my life. There was no doubt. Eugene told me that I had to love again. I had to let my heart love again, if I was going to be for Christ all that He wanted me to be. Eugene and Pat kept talking to me, and I knew it was the Lord speaking to me. On the long drive home, I kept telling the Lord He had to help me love and trust someone again. I couldn't do it on my own. I knew then why Robert kept calling me to see if I would make it. It was the Lord using Robert to get me there. God used Eugene and Pat to speak to me. We never know how God is going to work. He is always full of surprises.

There were a lot of people from Robert's past years of preaching at the anniversary celebration who were speaking. Toward the end of the service on Sunday, Robert got up and spoke to us. As Robert was speaking, he stopped for a minute. We could tell he was thinking about something. He said, "I am going to do it." He had a beautiful singing voice. Robert would bless us using the beautiful voice God had given him. He asked the piano player to please play a certain song for him. He sang for us, and it was beautiful. After he finished, he explained to us, the doctors had told him he should not sing or strain his voice. He could rupture vessels in his throat, and he would bleed to death. He said, he wanted to sing to his Lord one last time. If he died, it would be worth it.

It seemed the Lord's presence was in every minute of that trip. I had a long ride home to talk to the Lord and reflect on everywhere I was able to see Him. I really knew that the Lord had brought James and me together, and I was supposed to let the Lord's love pour out to James through me. It was going to be alright.

When I got back home, James and I talked, and I shared with him why the Lord had me make the trip back to Louisville to Robert's celebration. One thing I have always been able to do is be honest with James. James had told me over and over again that when he got to know me, he was praying that the Lord would use him to be my sounding board.

Not too long after this, the guy who had his cows on my place, began having medical problems. He was going to have to sell his cows. I was in the back yard one day when the gas meter reader came walking up to the back of the house to read the meters. I was usually at work when he came, so I had not talked to him before. He was friendly; we began to visit. He told me this sure was a pretty place. The farm is at the top of a hill and in my back yard looking to the east, there is a beautiful view of valleys and hills. I started telling him that I had a man who had cows here that helped keep the growth down, but he had to sell his cows because of his health. The meter reader told me his name was Richard. Richard told me that he and his son had sheep and cattle, and they were looking for a place to lease to keep some of their animals on. They did not live very far from where I live. Would I be interested in leasing some of the land to them? That sounded great to me. Help to maintain the farm was gone, but the Lord was going to bring what would turn out to be a double blessing to me. God is so full of surprises.

He brought his son back for me to meet. They seemed like really nice people, so we made an agreement for them to bring their animals to my farm. It was not long before I had meet most of their family, and we became friends. Nate, the son, was not afraid of Red my parrot. Most people like to look at him, but of all the animals on the place, he is the one no one wants to take care of. Parrots are beautiful birds, but with their bills they can inflict a terrible bite. The Lord had brought someone who wasn't afraid of Red, and he would be glad to look after the farm anytime I wanted to go away overnight or go home to visit family for a week. Who would have thought that when God shuts one door, He has a bigger and better one to open?

God is so good. He knows what we need. When we wait on Him and His timing, He will provide. It was like God had sent Richard and Nate into my life at the right time. James's dad and my father and step mom were still alive getting close to their 90's. James wanted his dad to meet me, and he lived in Gulf Shores. We had already established that our relationship would go by the Bible. There would be no intimacy before marriage. We would travel together as long as where we stayed could accommodate us in separate rooms. Poor James, some-times that meant sleeping on someone's couch, but he did not mind. When we were at his dad's he got the couch; at my kid's, he got the bed and I got the couch. I am little, couches are fine for me. James is six-feet-tall, but bless his heart he never complained.

We have laughed many times over the years James and I have been together. God really does have a sense of humor. I am from the North and Mr. James is from the Sothern hills of Tennessee. He has such a Southern accent, I had to really pay attention when he talked to under-stand him. I still have to have him repeat some words that I didn't quite get. I am short; Mr. James is tall; we both have white hair though. I like sweet cornbread; he likes unsweet. But what really brings us together is we both love the Lord, and His love flows through each of us to the other. He loves biscuits, and I do not make good ones, so although I love to cook, he has to make his own. The list of our differences goes on, but with the Lord in the center of our lives, it is these things that make us laugh, not build walls.

So, it was not much longer after getting to know Richard and Nate that we were off to Gulf Shores for me to meet James's dad. I really liked him, and he liked me. We stayed a couple of days with his dad and they took me all over the place. I had asked James if his dad, was saved. James said, "He was baptized in the Baptist church in Gulf Shores, after he had moved down there from East Tennessee." I felt the Lord speak to me that James's father needed praying for, because I had a feeling he was not saved. I thought "Oh, no, how am I going to tell James and his sister that their dad, who they think is saved, is not, and he needs to be prayed for?" We had a good time, and quickly it was time to head back home.

We had gotten a few miles down the road, when I knew I was being prompted to talk to James about his father, and I was going to lose my peace if I did not speak. I told James, "I don't know how to tell you, but we need to pray for your father. I do not think he is saved." James said, "I have seen the baptism papers." I told him, "That does not mean anything if he did not give his heart to the Lord." I told him what I had noticed, and from that day forward we began praying for his father.

It was getting close to Christmas, and I was invited to go with Mr. James to Tennessee to spend Christmas with Amy, James's sister, and his brother-in-law Bug and their family. James's dad would be there too. We would be back in time for my son and his wife to come in for the holiday. They came in when their work places gave them time off between Christmas and New Year's.

One night after James's dad, Grover, had gone to bed, we took Amy and Bug aside to share with them that the Lord had prompted me that we needed to pray for Grover. Amy shared she had always kind of wondered about his salvation. We had prayer for Grover, and then there were four of us praying for him. We had a great time, and I loved his family. Time passed quickly, and it was time to head back home to get ready for my son and his wife to come.

My son had been here once to meet James, and told me he was a keeper. Alison was going to get to meet him.

We had a good time, and soon it was time for my kids to leave and get back to the daily routine again.

James's eyes were not really good, so we spent a lot of time reading the Bible together. I would read it to him. And we would talk about it. James's eyes had a film built up, or, what he would eventually find out, was scare tissue that had built up from all the years of working in the fumes in the diesel mechanic shop. All the eye doctors he had gone to told him they were not able to help him. They said they did not think he could be helped. We made it a matter of prayer. I asked James to go to my eye doctor. I knew him because he went to Calvary Baptist Church where I was attending. He agreed to go.

Dr. Campbell looked at James and said, "I cannot help you, but I think I know an eye specialist who can." My eye doctor gave James Dr. Kim's name and number, and James called him and got an appointment. Dr. Kim examined James's eyes. Dr. Kim was the one who told James that he had scare tissue built up from working in all the fumes in the diesel mechanic shop. He knew of a compound that he could mix up. If he could still get the material that he could put on James eyes to soften the tissue, Dr. Kim could scrape it off.

It took three months for Dr. Kim to get the compound powders, but the office finally called James and said they were ready, if he was. He set up the appointments, one eye at a time. I took the day off to take James, as he had no family around here either to help him. He and his first wife had transferred to Alabama from Tennessee where they were both from, so that James could take the position of running the shop that he had managed for twenty-four years. I took James in, and when he came out after the scraping on one eye, he could really see me. I asked him, if he wanted to change his mind about me since he could now see clearly. He laughed and said that he was going to keep me. He said, "The scraping was really painful even though my eye was frozen." As the freezing wore off, it hurt even more. I had fixed food for him, so all he had to do was heat it up and eat. He stayed quiet because his eye hurt for a couple of days, but was also excited that he could see out of that eye. About two weeks later, James had his other eye done, and we were praising the Lord. After all those years of no hope of ever being able to see well again, his eyesight was restored. He just needed reading glasses. When people start to pray, God starts to work.

James's eyes were healed, and he could help me drive back to Michigan to meet my family. My son was flying me back and forth when I did get to go. But with James and I would be driving. Having a car there would make it a lot easier for us to go see other family members as my son and daughter live two and a half hours apart. My parents lived up near my daughter. They would not have to transport me around anymore. James and I had been seeing each other almost two years by this time.

This is how my Mr. James is. He wanted to ask me to marry him, but being that my father was still alive, he wanted to ask his permission-first before he asked me. My dad loved James right away; everyone does for that matter. James had just read a book about how it is a custom in some countries for a man to pay for the bride with a dowry. He had read normally it was five cows for a bride. It was ten cows for someone really special. James told dad that I was worth ten cows to him. My step mom was starting to go into dementia and she told Mr. James, "We are too old to take care of cows." Dad was so happy for us. We got to visit with everyone and headed home again. Everyone voted that Mr. James was a keeper.

I was still working at the bank. Somedays, God would bring someone for me to help pray through a circumstance in their lives, and then other days, Satan was trying to pound me into the ground. I had to stay until the Lord showed me something different. He was using that place where I had to take the abuse many times as a test to see if I would stay obedient, no matter what came at me. I knew I had to stay, but would I keep His Spirit or get angry and strike back? I would pray and ask for His Spirit to keep a tight grip on me.

It got close to two years to the day when Mr. James came to my house to talk to me. He had taken me out to dinner, and he looked at me and asked if I thought we could get engaged now? I looked at him and said, "Well, it's been two years, and you are still here. I guess we can." He told me he wanted me to pick out the ring, because I was the one who was going to be wearing it. I loved jewelry, and I loved diamonds. I had my mom's jewelry which came to me when she passed. The Lord was working on my heart and telling me to be humble. I had stopped wearing diamonds on most of my fingers. I was learning that His character was the only thing that was supposed to shine for people to see. I asked the Lord to show me what he wanted me to have. He gave me a vison of a ring. There was a jewelry shop that was advertised on the Christian radio station I listened to every day. I had a radio in the house, barn, and dog kennel, and I would hear this lady advertise their jewelry store. Not much of a shopper and fairly new to the area, I did not know where many stores were.

The day came when we decided to go out shopping for a ring. We were prepared for a whole day of shopping trying to find a ring. I had an idea of what I was supposed to get, but did not know how long it was going to take to find it. We decided to start at the jewelry store I heard advertised on the radio. We began looking at rings. The lady waiting on us was hauling out trays of rings, but none of them was what I felt that Mr. James was supposed to get me. I started describing what I was looking for, and the lady who owned the store was listening. She came over behind the counter and said, "Wait a minute, I think I have what you are looking for. I just got it in at an estate sale. It is still under the counter." She went over and pulled it out, and it was perfect. When she told us the price Mr. James couldn't believe it. He was expecting to have to pay twice as much as this ring cost. He said, "Are you sure?" I responded, "Yes, this was the exact ring what that Lord wanted me to have." We had a whole day planned out to shop, and here it was only a half hour and I had picked out the ring; it fit perfectly. We were walking out of the store. We had a whole day left.

Mr. James had it planned out where he was going to ask me to marry him. It was in another little town so he headed that way. There was an ice cream shop along the way. I did not know where he was taking me, but ice cream sure sounded good. They had three different kinds of sugar free ice cream, and when they asked me which I wanted, I said a scoop of all three. We ate our ice cream and were still praising God for how He had directed us to the exact place to get the ring. God had the exact ring hidden way back under a showcase, waiting for the time He would direct us to purchase the ring. James was beginning to learn how God works, and how He will guide His children when they really seek His will for their lives. I did not know it, but Mr. James was heading for a park called Spring Park, where there was a waterfall, to ask me to marry him and give me the ring. When we got there, there were people all over the place. By the time we parked the car and walked to the waterfall there was no one near the falls. Just God, Mr. James and I. We got in front of the waterfalls, and Mr. James got down on one knee, took my hand, and asked me if I would marry him. He was so precious. I said, "Yes." God had cleared that area for those few minutes for us to be alone there. When we were ready to leave the waterfalls, we saw people walking toward us coming to see the falls again. God is so amazing. We never know what He is up to next.

You have to remember Mr. James and I are in our late 60's. When we got in the car, Mr. James told me he had it planned out. He was going to get down on his knee to ask me to marry him, but his knees are not all that good from standing on concrete floors all those years. He knew the waterfalls at Spring Park had a railing in front of it he could use to help him get back up, if he could not get up alone. We had a good laugh over that one. He did make it back up on his feet on his own. The way he got up; I know the Lord gave Him a boost, at least that one time.

21

ENGAGED

Our families were excited that James and I had finally gotten engaged. We did not set a wedding day. I said I could not get married until I could spell his last name. His name is Robinette. It became a joke when people would ask us when we were getting married. We had talked about it; the Lord had made the arrangements for us to get together and planned the day we got engaged perfectly. We knew He would tell us when it was time to get married. After all, it was His plan not ours. Life has enough troubles of its own without trying to push ahead of the path the Lord has laid out for us to walk with Him.

Mr. James had started coming to church with me at Calvary. We were sitting in church listening to the pastor talk about a work and witness trip to Nicaragua. I felt the Lord tell me to go. I thought in my mind, "I don't have the money." The next thing the pastor said, "If you are holding back because you think you can't afford to go trust the Lord. He will provide." I am the one who likes to travel but not by myself. We had not been going to this church long, so I hardly knew anyone. James will travel, but he does not want to leave our country. I told James, "I think the Lord said to go." He said, "Then you need to go. I will take care of the farm."

I started attending the meetings. I began to get to know some of the people a little bit. The last meeting before we were to go, a lady came up and started talking to me. She was about my age, and I soon found out it was the pastor's mother. They lived an hour or so from here, but she loves to go on these trips with her son's church. The Lord had brought me a friend and one who was used to traveling this way. Finally, the day came to leave. The Lord was so faithful. He provided all the money I needed and extra so I could buy clothes. I bought clothes, wore them and when I left gave them to my interpreter's wife. All she had to do was wash them. She had new clothes, enough for a new outfit each day for a week.

Our church and pastor's friend in the ministry who had a church in South Alabama, had teamed up for our two churches to meet in Birmingham at the airport to make this trip together. There were sixty-four of us in all going. It took two compounds to house all of us when we got to our destination. The two compounds were only a couple of blocks apart.

The flight went well. We had to fly to Miami to go through customs and get on another plane to take us the rest of the way. The only problem was the pressure in the second plane must not have been right. Several of us started experiencing pain in our ears and head.

I sat next to a lady from the United States, who when we got to talking, was telling me about her daughter who was working in Nicaragua. She had gotten very sick and was in the hospital. The doctors did not really know what was wrong with her. She was flying down to Nicaragua to try to get her back to a hospital in the States, and she did not have a clue how she was going to do that. I told her, if she would like, I would pray with her for God's leading in the matter. I do not really know if she was a believer, but she accepted the prayer and thanked me for praying. Later, I prayed the Lord would let her see Him for the God that He is.

We landed and got off the plane. Those of us who had the ear problem could barely hear going into customs. I had not ever experienced this before when I flew. It kind of scared me. I did not know if it would be permanent or not. We had a medical team with us, and they had brought a lot of medical supplies to use when they set up in the different villages they planned on visiting. Customs did not want to release the medical supplies. It seemed like we sat there for hours. Finally, we got loaded on two buses. We found out that the medical supplies did not get to come with us. It would be a couple of days before they would find out if they could get them. We still had a couple of hours to ride, in buses, where we would stay for the time, we were there. It was already about 9:00 p.m. by the time we finally got to leave the airport, and we had-had nothing to eat since lunch.

We finally got to the compound where we would be staying. We pulled up to a place with huge thick high walls lined with razor wire all around the top. Well, I have a fence all around my place and my front yard is gated to keep my dogs in and other dogs out, but it is nothing like this. We were told we would be safe in here. It was pretty when we got inside. We saw beautiful flowing bushes and fruit trees. About midnight we had unloaded, and there was a meal waiting for us. We were to learn shortly that this was going to be our schedule for the rest of the week.

We had to pack lunches for the next day for sixty-four people. We prepared peanut butter and jelly for the regular workers, and lunch meat sandwiches for the guys on the building team. We had three teams who went in separate directions each day. These were the teams: eyeglasses, clothes distribution, medical and building. We saw each other for breakfast and evening meals. The medical team did not get to go out the first two days. They did not get their medical supplies until the second day. They had to be driven all the way back to the airport and sit and wait to get their medicines. It took most of the day for them. A lot of prayer was going up that they would be able to get the supplies.

Each day we went in a different direction about two to three hours away from our base. We were driven back into some villages that the people who lived there had never left. They walked or rode horses if they could afford one. It was beautiful country, and the people would be standing outside their homes waiting for us to get to their place to pray with them over their needs. I had two teens from our church and a young man who was our interpreter with me. At one village, one of the pastors from the village went with us. That was neat; we got to see things we would have never known to go see. The pastor led us through some woods to a beautiful flowing river where the women went to do their laundry. Out in the middle of the river were several huge, flat stones where the women could put their basket of clothes while they scrubbed their clothes on the stones.

In another village we were taken to where we would be bused away from the village and dropped off as a team. Each team was dropped off on different roads. We were told that if we saw any kind of path leading into the woods, to follow it, and there would be people somewhere along that path. I found a path and told the guys, "Let's go." We walked a long way, finally coming to a house. We had to cross a creek on a log. The people bathed in the water; we were told not to touch it. We could get sick. We met up with a pastor from the village back there. He was calling on the people. He asked us if we wanted to walk with him to see something. He led us to a forest of neatly planted trees. He explained it was a paint forest. The leaves, when squeezed were used to color paint. He walked along and would pick a leaf and squeeze it every few rows of trees. From a green leaf would come red, yellow, and blue. The pastor took us another mile back, and we came upon the most beautiful Brahma bull and cows I think I have ever seen. When we looked way off in a field with more cows in it, there was a cowboy on a horse galloping across the field.

Each night we held services back in the villages. After we had presented the gospel to the people when we were at their homes; we prayed with them, and they were invited to that evening's service in the village. I could not believe when evening came, here came people walking from every direction. I know how far some had to come. We had been to their homes. Most of the time church took place outside with the people sitting on plastic chairs. There were strings of lights the guys would put up that were run by a generator. The services would start about 6:00 p.m. and go until 9:00 pm. After the service we loaded up on buses for the haul back to the compounds; these people with their little children had the long walk back home in the dark through the wooded paths. These people were hungry for the word of God.

It was tiring, but the new challenge each day kept me excited and moving forward. The Lord had taken fear, away and I was enjoying the people who existed depending on the Lord each day. They were poor, but they have a freedom about them that we do not feel in the States where we have so much.

It was time to pack up and say goodbye to the people who took care of us when we were at the compound and those who had interpreted for us. We loaded up on the buses and headed back to the airport. This time it did not take so long. We passed through customs and got on the plane with no problems. The problems started when we hit a bad storm getting close to Miami, Florida. Our plane was being bounced around all over the place. People started screaming, "We're going to die." Someone else screamed, "There are too many Christians on this plane!" I thought, "You should be glad there are." Something I noticed was that I was not the least bit afraid. I felt a peace and a calm within. I was thanking the Lord that He had a hold of me.

We got close to Miami, and we were told that the plane was almost out of gas, and we couldn't land because of too much lightening. They were going to radio Fort Lauderdale and see if the airport would let us land there and fuel up, if we could make it that far. We got word they would let us go back and land in Fort Lauderdale, but we could not get off the plane because they could not handle international flights. They had no port of entry for people from other countries coming into the States. We started praying, and we eventually landed and the plane was fueled up. The airport let us sit and wait out of the way until the storm let up in Miami. It was raining in Fort Lauderdale without all the lightening.

We finally got word that the storm had let up enough for us to fly back to Miami. The pilot maneuvered the plane back on the runway, and we were taxing out to the takeoff runway. Suddenly, our plane jerked off to the right. Those on the left side of the plane could see what happened. A plane, coming in for a landing on the runway to our left, hit the runway and hydroplaned right toward our plane. That plane almost hit us. We were able to get back on the runway and go to the take off point. Finally, we got to the Miami Airport and safely landed. We were taken off the plane but could not go through customs without our baggage. We were all lined up waiting for our baggage, and we heard a loud thunder clap, and the power went down for a minute in the whole airport. This jammed up the conveyors that would bring our luggage from the plane to us. The power came back on, but the conveyors would not work. Workers were trying to fix the conveyors to get them to work again. By the time they got the conveyor fixed so we could get our luggage and get through customs, we were too late. The plane we were all supposed to be on had departed. Here we were, sixty-four people about midnight, in the Miami airport tired, hungry, with no place to go. The pastors started trying to get people rescheduled out to whatever flight they could get us on. We would have taken any flight that would take us close to where we lived.

We found one little food court a couple of terminals down from where we were. We were all able to get something to eat. Pastor put his mom and me with him and three other people as the last ones to fly out, so he knew everyone got out of the airport. We were all over the floor. Some were sitting, and some were curled up sleeping on their suitcases. Our flight was not until later the next morning. We decided to try and get a motel close by and at least get a little sleep. We found one and got a taxi to take us to the hotel. We got there about 3:00 a.m. The next day we found out there was a tram not far away from the hotel that we could use to take us to our terminal to fly out. The guys asked the hotel workers, if we could borrow their valet carts to get all our luggage to the tram. They said we could. Here we went. Now pastor's mother has lupus, and she was hurting pretty badly. She had her medicine, and she had to take it. It makes her groggy. We had to walk quite a way, cross a busy street about four lanes wide, and go up a fairly good-sized ramp to get to the tram. The guys had the luggage and Jean a nurse practitioner, and I were trying to get the pastor's mom safely to the tram. The tram only stops for a few minutes, and we had to get Donna on and sitting down before it took off. Talk about a trip to teach a person to pray non-stop; this was it.

It was the grace of God we made it. The tram stayed stopped at the airport a little longer for us to get off. We finally made it on the plane and back to the airport we had flown out of. Pastor's dad drove to that airport to take Donna home. The church had sent a van to get the rest of us. I was exhausted but praising the Lord all the way for His peace. I knew He was in control, and the trip was in His hands.

I was sixty-nine years old when I felt the Lord call me to go to a Bible college for a degree in preaching. This couldn't be. I thought, "I am too old. I can't do this." I would have to take online classes. The Lord and I discussed this for a bit. The Lord had spoken to me to drop back to part time at work. Now it made sense; this could be the reason to go to part time. When I checked in about the classes, I found out that we could only take one class at a time, and the class would require about thirty hours a week to do the work required. I said, "Father, I am sixty-nine years old; I can't do this." It was hardly an hour later I picked up a book I was reading and read, "The Lord does not call the equipped, He equips the one He calls." It made no sense to me, but I started the process to start classes. The Lord spoke; it was not for me to make sense of, but to obey.

The Lord was about to show, what an amazing God He is to me again. It was not long after starting these classes that I realized some of these students who were taking preaching classes, did not have a personal relationship with the Lord. This was not good. There was no doubt He was directing me what to write. I had class-mates from all over the world. When it came to writing a paper, I would have to get on the floor and tell God He had to tell me what to write. I had read all my assignments, but He was going to have to do the rest. I didn't have a clue where to start. He would tell me to get up and get to my computer. I would sit down, and I wrote what came to my mind. There were times when I got up the next morning and checked my emails and there would be a note from a student saying "I got it, I got saved last night. Jesus was with me. If I could jump through this computer, I would give you a hug." Being obedient is the key to seeing God work. In one class, several opened their hearts to the Lord. God is so amazing!

God always calls me to do what I cannot, so I must pray for Him to do it. When I know I can't do it, I stay out of His way and listen closely to what He tells me to do. Like the pharmaceutical sales lady I met at the hospital, I learned that God can use a person to reach someone else anywhere in the world, if it's His will.

I struggled all the way though school as a kid. I sometimes moved to three different schools in one year because of dad's work. In some schools I would be ahead, then I would and move somewhere else, and I would be behind. The best day of my life was when I gradu-ated high school. I never planned on attending college. I had completed four classes at Olivet Nazarene University when He shut the door. This time I had completed eleven Biblical classes when the Lord shut the door. It is more common for women to be preachers up North I have been told several times since moving to the South, "God does not call women to preach." Why He had me to take those classes, I am not really sure. I knew He got the grades; I didn't. My lowest grade was an "A-" in one class. The Lord never ceases to amaze me. He is so awesome. He did allow me to see another way He is in control of our lives.

It was early evening a few months after Mr. James and I had gotten engaged. James got a call from his father. His dad knew James would still be at my place, and he wanted to talk to both of us. He had called to tell us he had gotten saved. He was really saved this time. He confessed he had been living a lie all those years. When James and I had gone down to Gulf Shores for me to meet his dad, Grover did go to church with us. We attended a church he would attend when he did go to church. James knew the people and the pastor there. James's dad had called James's sister and husband to share the good news with them. I can tell you, the angles in heaven where not the only ones rejoicing over one more soul making it into the family of God.

That fall Grover started not feeling well. He was able to keep his place up, go fishing off the pier in Gulf Shores anytime he wanted to, and do pretty much anything he wanted to do up to this point. Grover had a doctor who lived right by him who had been good friends with the family for years. Dr. McCollough was really good about running up to visit with Grover several times a week before heading to his clinic which was close by where they lived. Amy and James would talk to their dad every night before going to bed.

It was January when Grover began having medical problems. James was going to go down and stay with his dad for a week. He was going to pack enough clothes to last him a week, and I felt that he might need to pack more clothes in case he needed to stay longer. I told him not to worry; I would look after his dogs and house. He listened to me.

The morning that James was to leave to go to Gulf Shores, I woke up in awful pain and was very sick to my stomach. I called James and told him. He came as quickly as he could get here. I was on the floor doubled up in pain and had the dry heaves. He called the emergency room where my doctor was, and they told him to bring me right in. It was a twenty-five-mile drive to the hospital and James was praying all the time he was driving me to the hospital. When we got to the emergency room, James went in for help. When they came out and saw me, I did not have to wait to be admitted. James filled out paperwork for me and then came back where I was. They gave me something that took the pain away, and then they took me for x-rays. I had kidney stones, and one was traveling. I had never had them before. I must have passed one, but they told me I was full of them and I would be back. James took me home and headed for Gulf Shores.

I knew God was in control and he had James there when I needed him. I have been told when I have had x-rays that they can see I have them, but I have never been bothered since that one time, thank the Lord. God let me see He will provide what we need when we need it, just in time.

James ended up being with his dad in Gulf Shores from January through April. By this time Grover was getting better. James's sister was able to go down and spend a few weeks with their dad, so James could come home.

Grover got better and was able to stay on his own again. The doctor made sure he checked in on Grover morning and night. The doctor had a key to the house, and one morning he went to check on Grover. He had to let himself into the house. When he went to look for Grover, he found him on the floor at the foot of the bed. It looked like Grover had gotten up and was going to the bathroom and passed.

When James got the call from Dr McCollough, we were broken-hearted but praising God at the same time. God is so good. He inspired us to pray; prayer set His Holy Spirit to work in Grover's heart. We may not have Grover with us here today, but we will have eternity to spend with him.

James packed up to head back to Gulf Shores. I did not go. He was going to be there for some time again. James would have his family with him down there through this rough time. I had to work, and I would take care of his animals and place. James got to talking with the pastor from the church where Grover had attended. He told the family that he saw a big change in Grover after he gave his heart to the Lord. He was not in church only when he felt like it; he was in church every time the doors were open. When we surrender our lives to Jesus, people will notice.

I was still working at the bank, and the pressure was great. There was a person trying to get me fired. She did not like it that I was a Christian. I was taken aside and told I could not mention Jesus around this person. There were people who would share with me their situations and ask me to pray with them. I would meet them in the bathroom, or at the Dollar General Store next to where we worked. We were allowed to go to on our breaks. I would meet them there and pray with them. This person sat about six feet from me at her desk. I could not say, "Good morning," to this person. This person thought that I was just too happy when I came to work in the mornings. This person had a lot of stress at home, and I knew it. I prayed hard for her.

I was still reading *Streams in the Desert* every morning in my devotion time. God kept this book in my hand to keep me grounded, or I probably would have hit the ceiling. I was constantly being reminded that there is a divine mystery about suffering. We can't understand it, but there is supernatural power attached to suffering. If we are going to develop a deep level of spirituality or holiness, we are going to suffer deep trials. I was seeing in my life, what the Lord could do through a person who was seeking Him with all of his heart. I had asked Him to let me see what He could do with a person who surrendered his life completely to Him. I have never forgotten asking Him to show me this. I know He had put the determination in my heart to walk deeper into the flames with Him, no matter what. I had read that if we hold on and allow the Lord to put us through the refining process, a peace and calm will come to us that the world knows nothing about. I was beginning to understand how wonderful that could be to live a life like that. I wanted that peace and calm. The disciples had it, and they were just ordinary men. And as I went through each storm, I was beginning to focus my attention more on God. I was beginning to look for how was He going to get the glory on the other side of this storm.

It was a Friday, the co-worker, who was giving me such a rough time, and I had to stuff a whole box of mail into envelopes. We were working off the same stack of envelopes. My hand brushed her hand when we both reached for an envelope at the same time. That did it. She exploded at me. I had deliberately pushed her hand. I was being called every nasty thing under the sun that she could think to say. Finally, she ran out of things to call me and stopped. I stood there looking at my co-worker thinking, "I feel a calm I have never felt before." As she was raging on at me, I was thinking, "Wow! This is not me. Father, it has to be You." When my co-worker finally stopped trashing me, I remember asking her very calmly, "Don't you have anything else? Get it out. It doesn't matter what you say to me; I am going to love and pray for you anyway." That was the Lord speaking through me. I was still in wonder at the peace and calm I was feeling. These words never came to mind to say, but God gave me the words that came out of my mouth. I went home and cried and really prayed for this person.

Monday morning, I was sitting at my desk when my co-worker came in to work. I didn't dare look at her or say a word. I had been told I was not to. The next thing I knew, a hand came on my shoulder. My co-worker leaned down, and in a low voice said, "I am so sorry. I have been so mean to you. Can you every forgive me?" She was forgiven. We both cried, and we became friends.

With my last husband I was held to the flame for fifteen years. With this person I was held to the flame for a year before the Lord changed the circumstance. The Lord took away my husband, but God worked the opposite with my co-worker. We became friends. We never know how He will work, but, in His time, He does. Through this trial I got to see how much the Lord had worked on me, as well as, what He did in my co-worker's life. Each trial was teaching me more about the power of persistent prayer. Prayer will change me, as well as, it changes others.

James and his family ended up staying a month or so when they went back to Gulf Shores for their dad's funeral. Their dad was the type to keep every piece of paper, nut, bolt, and screw he had ever gotten. He had a huge building outside packed with things along with smaller outside buildings packed full. James, his sister and her husband started wading through the buildings. James and Amy started trying to sort out and get rid of what they did not want to keep themselves. James has a tendency to be like his father. I had moved seven times in fifteen years. The Lord had taught me to hang on to material things with loose fingers. Every time I had to pack up things, things began to have less meaning to me.

As they began to clean out these buildings, James would call me and ask if I wanted this or that. I told him, "No, I do not want anything." Much of what James's dad had treasured had deteriorated. Piles of lumber was eaten by termites, and metal items had rusted. This shows that earthly things don't last; the things of God last eternally.

James, his sister and husband worked hard to dispose of their dad's property.

James had to come home for doctors' appointments. Amy and Bug stayed on to continue working. James's dad lived about four miles straight in from the ocean. A storm came that brought water inland, flooding James's dad's property. This was unusual for the flooding to get that far inland. It was a good thing Amy and Bug were there to sand bag the house. What the termites, rot and rust did not destroy, the flood washed away. James learned a lesson. James told me he realized what the Bible said about storing our treasures on earth. We need to concentrate on storing our treasures for heaven.

22

GOD'S PERFECT TIMING

By now James and I had dated two years, and were engaged for three years. We felt the Lord letting us know it was time to get married. We knew when we got married, we would live at the farm. James had shared with me that he had always wanted to have horses and live on a farm. We prayed about it asking the Lord to sell James's place. We would get married when the Lord sold James's house. He listed his place for sale by owner and started sorting, giving away things and packing what he wanted to keep. Like I said, "He is a little like his dad."

We had talked and figured that if he sold his house, he would have thirty days to get out. We were planning on having the pastor marry us. We didn't want a big affair. So that should not be a big deal. With the Lord's help we could do it.

The house was for sale a few weeks when James got a call from a realtor. There were a couple of young people they had known all their lives who were getting married. The realtor thought that James's house would be perfect for them. The guy's parents were no longer living, and there was no one to help them. If James would let this realtor handle the selling of the house to these kids, they would not charge James anything. That way the house would be less expensive for the kids to buy if there was not a realtor's fee added to it. James said, "Yes, that will be fine."

The realtor brought the kids out, and they loved the house. James had a fenced-in backyard, and the young man had a big dog. It was perfect for them. Yes, they wanted the place.

Now my place is stuffed with furniture. There is not room for anything. We talked about it, and this young couple just starting out had nothing we were told. We felt the Lord impress on us to give them the furniture and dishes, even the china dishes in the china cabinet. They couldn't believe it. We were thrilled. We did not have to pack or move anything. James had moved a lot of things here already. He pretty much needed to pack his clothes and his dogs and come.

We started telling people we were getting married and had set a date. Friends started telling us we could not be married unless they could be there. We had been together for five years; they wanted to see us get married. Oh dear. We had thirty days to plan a wedding and small reception. Lord, help us. He did. People started telling me what they wanted to do. One of my co-workers baked cakes, and she made our wedding cake; I made some food. Others volunteered to make food and some of my co-workers served the food. The church was open, so we could be married in the sanctuary and have an area in the fellowship hall for the reception after.

I had to get a dress to be married in. I was told about a couple of places where I might find what I needed. I started out one day to go shopping thinking it would be an all-day project. In the second store, a lady came up to help me. The store was full of dresses. I really do not like to shop all that much. I told her I needed a dress to get married in. I needed something with color. She went and brought me a beige dress. I told her tan and beige made me look like a dead person walking. She looked at me and I thought, "Okay, I will try it on for her." I walked out of the dressing room for her to see how the tan dress looked on me. She looked at me and said, "you get it off, I will be right back." This time she came back with the prettiest light teal dress. I tried it on. It did not need much done to it to make it fit. The shoes were right there beside the dressing room; they went perfectly with the dress. As I was checking out, she showed me a box of earrings, and there were the perfect earrings to go with it all. God was in it. I was in and out in forty-five minutes and off to get the rest of the supplies I needed for the wedding.

We had the wedding planned, and James moved a few days before we got married. He stayed at a motel a couple of miles from the farm. My son flew in and spent a couple of days with us. Alison, my daughter-in-law wanted to come, but she was too far along with our grandson, and the airlines said she could not fly. A pastor friend and his wife from Kentucky came in for a couple of days ahead, and they helped us prepare food and set up at the church. They stayed at the house too. Amy and Bug drove across the day of the wedding. God was showing us that nothing is impossible for Him. He brought the people needed to get everything done. I had made friends when I first started at Calvary with a lady named Nita, who had worked for a decorator for years. She made all my flower arrangements. My daughter and family wanted to be at the wedding, but with the farm and what they have going on, they can only leave at certain time. This was not a good time for them.

We made it to the wedding day; all was ready to go. There were a lot of people there to make sure we really did get married. When we reflect back, only the Lord could have made all this happen in thirty days with such precision.

Shortly after Mr. James and I had gotten married we had to get hay for the horses. We could not find any square bales so we had to get big round bales. We did not have a tractor to help handle these bales, so we had to try and move them by man power. I was born with a double curvature of the spine. That was one reason I rode Paso Fino horses most of my life. They have a very smooth gate and did not jar my back when I rode. I had also fractured my back a couple of years before when I slipped on black ice on the back deck. I have always worked hard all my life and didn't think twice about pushing on one of those big bales of hay to get it off the trailer. I heard and felt something happen again in my back. There was pain again, I thought, "Well, I have been here before; I will get better."

Not too much longer after this incident, I had reduced back to working part time at the bank. I worked afternoons every day. James and I had been shopping in the morning, and he had dropped me off at work. He would come back and pick me up that night. When I left work, it was dark outside. When I went to get in the truck, I stepped on a good-sized stone that I did not see. It twisted my knee and my back in such a way, that both my knee and back were in instant pain. I felt sick to my stomach. Instantly I could hardly walk or move without pain I could hardly stand or move. Mr. James jumped out of the truck and got ahold of me and helped me into the truck. I could not stand to bend my left knee. It was so painful to get in the truck. I did not want to go to the hospital. I just wanted to go home so I could lay down.

The next day I was still in such pain I called my doctor. I got in right away to see him. He sent me for x-rays. The x-rays let them see I had several fractures in my back that must have happened before. The doctor gave me some pain medicine and anti-inflammatories that were supposed to help. The medicine broke me out into those horrible hives I had had many years ago. I could not take anything he tried to give me. Another kind of medicine broke me out in big sores all over my body. My doctor was a Christian and we talked about the Lord a lot. Finally, I told him, "I believe the Holy Spirit that resides in me is objecting to what you are having me put into this body." The pain medicine was strong and was a narcotic. I have always tried to stay away from strong medicine. I had seen enough of what it could do to people.

The nurse called me one day and said, "The doctor has ordered for you to go and have an epidural, a shot into the spine that should help relieve your pain." I was not going to let them put a shot in my spine. After I hung up from talking to the nurse, I thought that was strange. Something inside me was so determined I should not get that shot. It must have been the Holy Spirit. I told Mr. James about it. The nurse was a little upset with me for refusing the procedure. She said, "Well, it will get rid of your pain for you." The doctor prescribed a medication for that was in the shot that they wanted to give me in my spine. I was to take it by mouth. I took two pills, and I woke up in the middle of the night with horrible stomach pains, weeping sores; I was a mess. My back was killing me. My knee swelled up the night of the incident and was still swollen huge. Now I had horrible stomach pains, and sores coming all over my body. Finally, the doctor sent me to Vanderbilt Hospital in Nashville to the spine clinic.

It took a little while, but I got in. I had to lie across the back seat of the truck. I could not stand to sit up for very long. I had been pretty much living in our Lazy Boy chair all this time. When we got to Vanderbilt, and I got to see the doctor; he examined all my records. I told him about the doctor back home wanting to give me an epidural, and that I refused it. Then I told him about the medication the doctor at home had given me and the reaction I had to it. I had taken pictures of the sores on my body. I was able to show him what I looked like. The doctor looked at me and said, "It is a good thing you did not take that shot. You would have been dead by now or paralyzed for the rest of your life." I knew than it was the Holy Spirit speaking to me that day. They did MRIs on my back and leg. The doctor told me he could do a procedure on my back to kill the nerves, but that was all that they could do for me. I have osteoporosis in my back and hips, and surgery of any kind is out of the question. My bones would fall apart.

The doctor did a procedure on my knee to see if it would bend if he froze it. When he put the needle in my knee, it felt like it went all the way through my leg. I about came off the table. When he was telling me what it would be like going in the spine to kill the nerves, he said it would be about like what he had done to my knee. They would have to go in one time and freeze different areas to find out where exactly the spots were that were causing the pain. Then I would have to go back, and they would kill the nerves. I know the body can repair itself, and I asked him, "Wouldn't this have to be done more than once?" He said, "Yes." He had learned a procedure that would last a few years longer than the one that most doctors do. I told him, "If it was like what happened with my knee it did not sound too good." He told me, "Well, I am not too good on selling it either."

He referred me to a knee specialist closer to home. I went to him, and he said I pretty much needed both knees replaced. He gave me a huge cortisone shot in my knee. It took my swelling down, and I was awake for three days and three nights because of the shot. I have had to take so much cortisone in the past for my hives, it really affects me now when I have to take it. If I could have walked and gotten around, I could have cleaned my house from top to bottom. I was so charged up from the shot. After three months of not being able to bend my knee, I could bend it again. I could walk for as long as my back could stand for me to be in an upright position.

I pretty much lived in my Lazy Boy recliner for three months. I had my Bible, devotionals, journals and books packed around me. I had a lot of time and I took advantage of it to spend time with and seek the Lord. One night I was in a lot of pain and could not sleep. The Lord came to me and asked me, "What if I leave you this way the rest of your life?" At this point it looked like it was going to be my fate for the rest of my life. Believing God to be sovereign, I thought that if this is how He chose to leave me, it was His will for my life. After all He did create me for His purpose.

After about three months I was able to go back to church with lots of pillows. We had a guest minister come to speak. I knew him from hearing him on the radio each day. I loved to hear him. He had been told about me, and at the end of the service he anointed me with oil and prayed for God to heal me. When he had finished, he said to me, "Now don't look for the healing today. It's out there, but you have to get to it." As many books on prayer as I had read, I had not heard we had to get to the healing. But I never forgot those words. In time the pain got less, and I could start getting around. I am so thankful to my God; I know if I had an x-ray my back would still look a mess. The way I can get around and do things in the house and outside on the farm, I know without doubt, God is holding me. I should not be doing what I am able to do and taking no medication. We read that God is in control of our very breath. He has made it so I do not take such things for granted. I know every step I take is in His power, not mine.

We had gotten married in August, and it was Thanksgiving when I got a call that my stepmom slipped and had fallen down their basement stairs. She had shattered her right elbow and hit her head on the concrete floor at the bottom of the stairway and had a concussion. I called my son and told him what had happened. He got me a flight out on Thanksgiving Day, but I would have a layover in Atlanta, Georgia. I would also have to change terminals. I would be flying alone. I had been in the Atlanta airport, one time, years ago with my mother. She flew all the time in and out of that airport going to Florida to see her parents. She knew the airport well. All I had to do was follow her to get where we needed to be.

I was going to have to fly this time alone. I threw myself at the Lord and told Him I was trusting Him to help me make it through the changes. After landing in Atlanta, I was told I would have to go downstairs, catch the right tram to the terminal I needed, and get off at the right place. I did not have any time to linger; I would have to hurry. The Lord is so faithful. I got to talking to the lady sitting on the plane beside me, and she said, "I know where you need to be. I get off the terminal before yours. You go with me, and when I get off, the next time the door opens you get off." The Lord did it again. He took care of me. When I got to the Detroit airport, my son was waiting for me. Was I ever glad to see him.

He took me to the rental place the next morning early and helped me get a rental car. I was going to need a car to get around going back and forth to the hospital. I was able to stay at my daughters to sleep, but since Mom hit her head, she had to have someone with her, if she was not sleeping. She could not have surgery on her arm for a couple of days, until they knew the activity going on in her brain was stable enough so that she could be put to sleep for the surgery.

Mom spent a week in the hospital, and I stayed with her except to go to Missy's to sleep. My sister had our dad who was in a wheel chair because his spine had collapsed and he could not walk. Dad was in his 90's and with all the trauma he went through, his mind was failing him also. My sister lived two hours from the hospital and would get dad up to see mom, but he could not handle being there for any length of time.

Mom ended up in a nursing home, and I spent every day with her for the first week. The social worker at the hospital said it would be easier on Mom with the way her mind was, if someone was there with her as much as possible for at least a week. Work gave me another week off, and I stayed. Dad and Mom both grieved not seeing each other. They had been together for so many years. Eventually, Mom was moved from the rehab part of the nursing home to a resident room, and Dad was able to go with Mom.

I had been driving a pick-up truck for years. With the horses and animals, I needed a truck. My son got me a little car to get around in from the rental place. The gas mileage was great, and I forgot how easy a little car was to park. It was actually easier for me to get in and out of. I did not have to pull myself up to get in the car like I did the truck. I had no problems getting in the truck until my back went down on me.

When I got home, I said something to James about possibly getting a little car. He had about run the wheels off his vehicle driving back and forth to come to my place to see me every day for four years and to Gulf Shores to be with his dad. We knew we had to have a truck, and James told me he would really like to have my truck to drive. We decided to sell his Envoy, and I would look for a little car. I started praying about it when I was still back in Michigan, "Lord if this is You putting it on my heart to have a little car, lead me to the car you want me to have." I had a vison of a little red car.

It was the first day of December, and I had a dentist appointment in Muscle Shoals. I left work to go to my appointment and was heading back to work after my dental visit. I drove past a car dealer, and there sat the cutest little red car. It sat there in the middle of a whole row of cars right out front. I thought, I will stop for a second and see about the car. Three salesmen came out right away. Of course, they wanted to take me in and talk to me about it. They would have to look up the information. I did not have time to stay; I had to go back to work. They told me there was a really good deal on that car, and it would not be there long. They told me, "If you think you want it, you better come in right now." I looked at the three of them and told them, "I believe God is in control, and if He wants me to have that car, it will be here when I can get here again." They did not know what to say, other than, "Have a good day."

I got so busy; I really did not think much about the car. It was getting close to the holidays, and I had a lot to do. Christmas was over, and it was the last day of the month. James and I decided we needed to go to Sam's Club about thirty miles from our place. There is more than one way to get there. We took one way to get there, and on the way home I thought about the car. I said to Mr. James, "Do you want to see the car I was telling you about?" He did, so we drove by way of the car lot to go home. Sure enough, one month later, there sat that little red car in the same place I had seen it before. This time it was the only car. This time there were trucks lined up along the front row.

We went in to talk to someone about it. I was not looking for anything special except that it has a large enough trunk for our luggage when we traveled. We looked in the trunk. Yes, there was plenty of room. We went in this time to find out about how much the car was. I knew how much I could afford for a car payment. The salesman started telling us this was really a good deal. The car was bought brand new, and the person only drove it for 3,000 miles, and brought it back for a bigger car. The price was dropped several thousands of dollars. There was a special going on because it was the last day of the year, and they wanted to move some cars off the lot to bring in new ones. By the time I walked out, I had an almost brand-new Corolla for exactly what I had in mind for a car payment, including an extended warranty. James drove the truck home with the groceries, and I drove home in that new little red car. The Lord had left it on the lot for a whole month, so that I could get back and buy it. It was an exceptional deal and it should have sold. But I have learned if the Lord wants me to have something, it will be.

Ten years before buying this car, I had bought my truck. God had done the same thing more or less when I bought it. I needed a truck. I did not care if it had roll-up windows. I needed a truck. He brought me a new Chevy Silverado that had been impounded. I was told that it is almost impossible to buy a vehicle from a lot that has been impounded. The salesman I bought the truck through found me discounts, and I believed cut into his commission to make it possible for me to buy this truck. It was when it was a really bad time for car sales. He brought the truck to my door. He knew how much I could afford for a payment. The payment worked out to exactly what I had to spend. God has blessed me so much more than I deserve. How can I not surrender my life to Him every day and obey when He tells me to do something? I get to see Him work everywhere in my life as well as other's lives.

Every spring and fall I usually get to go back home and see the family. When spring came and it was time to go to see family, we packed up and headed out in my new little red car. It was comfortable and after driving a truck for so many years, I loved how economical the car was on gas. I loved driving the car. We spent our week getting to see all the family. We always go to my son's first in Livonia, Michigan three days. On Wednesday morning, we pack up and head toward my daughter's. We stopped at the nursing home to have lunch with Dad and Mom and spend the afternoon with them. About the time my daughter's family is getting home from work and school, we leave to go stay with them the last few days. It is about a 45-minute drive back to the nursing home from my daughter's, so we went back a couple more times to see my parents and spend a few hours with them.

Dad was not feeling well when we were there this time. Some years ago, dad was supposed to have surgery on his spine because it was collapsing. They discovered prostate cancer and never did do the spine surgery. He was given forty-two radiation treatments that killed the cancer but caused a lot of other problems. He had to be put in the hospital a few of times due the complications. We did not know if this condition was causing him trouble now or not. Dad kept saying there was something wrong, but he did not know what. The doctor at the nursing home was supposed to be checking things out with dad.

Mr. James asked my dad one of the days we were there with my parents, "Vic, are you alright with the Lord?" I know when they were able to see well enough to read Mom and Dad would sit and read the Bible. When they could not read anymore, I got them the Bible on CD for them to listen to. I really did not know where my dad stood with the Lord. Dad told James he was saved. I was out of the room with Mom when James talked to my dad. Mom's mind had gotten a lot worse since the last time I saw her. We could be talking with her, and she would get up and walk out of the room, not really having anywhere in mind she was going. James told me that he had talked to my dad on our way back to my daughter's that evening.

On Friday nights usually Rod, Alison and our grandson Brandon come to Missy's and Marc's to spend the night and we get to spend Saturday as a family together. Sunday morning, about 4:00 a.m. we get up for the 14-hour drive back to Alabama. It is a busy week with a lot of driving, and we usually get home exhausted. We had a good time, but I was still working, so I had to go to work the next morning at 8:00 a.m.

We had not been home two days when I got a call at work from my sister. She had gotten a call from the nursing home in the night; Dad was not doing too well. By morning Dad had passed away. She called to tell me Dad had passed. We had to pack back up and head back to Michigan again. God's timing is always perfect. He had gotten us there so we were able to spend time with Dad before he passed. God also knew we would need that little car, and He got it to us just in time. Gas was so expensive at this time.

I have shared with you how God worked miracles to save my life, and how He has provided what I needed when I needed it. He loves us so much; He really does care about the little things in our lives. It makes me sad when I hear people tell me, "Oh, I don't bother God with little things. He is too busy to be bothered with such things." The Bible says, *(Psalms 37:4-Take delight in the Lord and He will give you the desires of your heart. NIV)*. He does care, He has shown me time and again that He cares about the little things, as well as, the big. *(Philippians 4:6 Don't worry about anything, but in everything, through prayer and petition with thanksgiving, present your requests to God. CSB)*.

The year 2018 was a busy year for Mr. James and me. The Lord had spoken to me to quit work. I really had no intentions of quitting work, until I could not get out of bed to get there. I had worked all my life doing something; I was not about to stop now. I was down to part time each day, and that was good. Now He had shut the door at work. "Now what," I wondered.

Our church had a mission that distributed food, clothes and household goods to people in our county. It is a good-sized mission, and it takes lots of hands to keep it going. James had been volunteering there for several years. I was not working anymore. I felt the Lord speak to me, "You have time, so you can go and help." I started going each week. We would spend about twenty hours a week working at the mission. Our church, which is a pretty-good-sized church for our area, had not had a library for several years. I am a reader. The Lord was putting the right books in my hands to read to help me to grow. If He could do this for me through books, He can do this for anyone. Mr. James and I asked our pastor about starting a library at our church, and Brother Wade agreed. Mr. James was willing to help me. We had donated books, purchased books, and, within a year, we had almost a thousand books on the shelves for people to check out.

God was so good; He knew I would have trouble adjusting to not working, and He put me to work for Him. After a year at the mission, we settled down to taking care of the farm and putting our energy in the library.

The spring of 2019 has been totally different for us. This was the first spring I had not been working at a job for years. The young man, who has his cattle and sheep on our farm, also raises all kinds of chickens, quail and Guineas at his place. I had gotten a couple of chickens from my daughter in Michigan and brought them home with two Nigerian pygmy goats. Nate said to me, "Vicki you need some Guineas on this place. They eat ticks, fleas and all sorts of bugs."

I forgot to tell you, ticks and fleas, as well as, fire ants are terrible here. My first encounter with fire ants was just the beginning. I love being outside, but would come in every night in the summer covered in bites from something. We always had to check ourselves for ticks. For some reason I get bitten more than anyone I know. If there was something that would eat these bugs, I was all for it. Nate brought me six tiny week-old baby keets, (This is what Guineas are called when they are babies.) It was so much fun watching them grow.

Over my life I had delivered puppies, foals, rabbits, and lamas, but I had not seen with my own eyes a bird hatch. I had slept in the barn with my miniature horse mares due to give birth, because the babies often do not come out of the sack without someone to break it for them. A miniature foal could drown in the umbilical fluid if it does not break through the sack soon enough. What I had never seen, other than in pictures, was a bird hatch.

The Guineas I had raised the year before started laying eggs. A hen had decided to sit on her eggs. They are free to go all over the farm to eat bugs, so we have to go look for the nests. I found where she had laid her eggs, and we started watching her. One day I went to check her, and there beside her was a little keet that had hatched. A little while later there was another one. I knew she had a lot more eggs under her. I kept a close watch on her all day expecting to see some more little one's hatch. She would leave her nest each day but not for long, to get a drink and something to eat. Later in the day she left her nest with her two babies. I kept waiting for her to go back and sit on her eggs.

I had been told that when baby chicks or birds are about ready to hatch, they can be heard peeping inside the egg. Pretty soon they will start cracking the egg. It was about a 100-degree day. I knew the eggs would still be kept warm even if mom was not on the nest. A couple of hours later mom still was running all over with her two babies. I went to check the nest. I could not believe it. I heard a peeping sound. I picked up the egg I thought it was coming from, and it peeped again. There was another baby coming, and mom was not the least bit interested in her nest anymore. I collected all the eggs that were left in the nest and brought them in the house. I put all the other eggs in a box with a light, but held this one in my hands to keep it warm. That day the Lord gave me my heart's desire. It was not long and the baby keet was breaking the shell. In an hour or so I had a baby keet born in my hand. I knew it was God. He can engineer anything He wants to make happen.

When we seek Him with all of our heart, He will give us the desires of our hearts. Nothing is too small or too big for Him to bring, but there is a condition, our desires must match up with His desires. God works in ways that are going to bring Him the honor. We must have the Holy Spirit residing in us so that His desires become our desires. God really does want to show Himself to His children and let us see Him for the majestic God He is.

The Lord not only fulfilled a desire of my heart, but I was going to learn a lesson from this little keet being born. This was the summer of 2020. We had COVID- 19 released upon us.

The next thing we knew the county was being told we must wear masks everywhere we go. It was not long and churches were shut down. The Lord has commanded us in, *(Hebrews 10: 24, And let us consider how we may spur one another on toward love and good deeds, (25) not giving up meeting together, as some are in the habit of doing, but encouraging one another –and all the more as you see the Day approaching. NIV)*. Here we were not allowed to meet. Calling friends from the church and talking to them, I could hear the despair in some of their voices. It had come to mind that the evil one is working on suppressing God's children. Satan's goal is to discourage and undermine our effectiveness by keeping us from other believers. He knows it will be more difficult to counteract the ungodly messages of the world when we are held in isolation, which will make God's children an easy target for the enemy.

What I had learned from this one little Guinea was, it had come out of its shell fine, but it would not eat. I put food and water right in front of it. I went out on U-Tube to see what I could find about how I might be able to get this little one to eat. What they showed me to do, did not work. I texted Nate who was still at work and told him my situation. He said he had a batch of eggs hatch the day before in his incubator. Right after work he would bring me some of his baby keets to put with this little one. I kept trying to get my little keet to eat until Nate could get some other keets here. Finally, here he came with five more to go with this one. I could not believe it, as soon as those other keets were placed in the cage with the single one, my little keet went over and started eating with the others. Alone with food and water right in front of it, my little keet would have starved to death. There was something about being in a community that stimulated the keet to eat. They are all still running in their own little group healthy, happy and almost grown.

God has created His children the same way. We are made to be in community. His church was intended to keep his community together to feed us and keep us focused on the Bread of Life, so that we would stay spiritually healthy. We must stay connected, first with the Lord, and then with each other.

You may be thinking, "What I can do? I am a nobody." When we really get an understanding of how God works, it is the ones who know that they need the Lord, who are the ones He can use. When we get to see Who He is and what He can do, there is nothing on this earth to compare to the blessing we get to share in with our Lord. He gets all the credit because it is all about Him. His blessing spills over on us and then over onto others. We get to see our sovereign Lord at work in us, through us and around us. Might I say that when He opens our eyes to see, our ears to hear and our hearts to obey, we get to see our Lord in a way that the majority of the people will never see.

He puts us through the fire to clean self out of us, so He, through the Holy Spirit, can live His life through us. We are to be Jesus in the flesh to people who are not walking close to Him yet. Jesus uses our feet to come to them, our arms to reach out to them, and our mouths to speak to them. We may be led by the Spirit to do what self would say no to. God knows this, this is when He knows we must be led through the refining fires until self is gone, and Jesus comes shining through.

Something I am learning is that saving grace is free. All we have to do is realize we are born sinners and we need a Savior. Ask Him to come into our hearts, knowing we need Him. What I have learned is if we want to see miracles, it is going to cost. We have to give up something to see miracles. I have noticed in some translations of the Bible the word "fasting" has been taken out. Satan does not want us to know about the fact there is power released in suffering for the sake of our Lord. I have seen it time and again, when people are willing to fast and spend time in prayer, God works.

There is another reason the Lord may allow us to go through different forms of suffering. *(Streams in the Desert: July 19 - In order to have a sympathetic God, we must have a suffering Savior, for true sympathy comes from understanding another person's hurt by suffering the same affliction. Therefore, we cannot help others who suffer without paying a price ourselves, because afflictions are the cost, we pay for our ability to sympathize. Those who wish to help others must first suffer. If we wish to rescue others, we must be willing to face the cross; experiencing the greatest happiness in life through ministering to others is impossible without drinking the cup Jesus drank and without submitting to the baptism*

He endured… The school of suffering graduates' exceptional scholars.)

I am a nobody, but I have gotten to see what my Lord can do. He had to take "self" out of me so that He was able to take me into situations and circumstances that I would not have walked into, if I had not surrendered my life to the Lord. He had put these books into my hands to help me understand what was going on in my life, and even though it hurt, to keep hanging on to Him. I would get to see for myself how God is still working in our day like He did in the days we read about in His word. I have had the privilege to watch Him not only transform my life, but He has brought others into my life, whom I would have never gotten near, and allowed me watch them be transformed by His amazing grace.

Journaling what I see God doing in my life and around me makes me more aware of how He works. It seems like when I feel Him direct me to pray and fast for a personal cleansing, I start looking for what He might be up to. You see, He has to have a clean vessel to work through. In our homes, we can clean one day, but the next day clutter and dust starts creeping back in. I will pick up my house and keep it up daily, but if I am going to have people in for a special occasion, I will give it a deeper cleaning than I do on a daily basis. Until Jesus comes and establishes His throne on a new earth, we will have to ask God to search us daily. Little issues and attitudes build up. If He is going to really show Himself through us or Himself to us, He will call for a little deeper cleansing. This takes fasting and praying.

It has been when God's church will humble themselves, fast and pray that we see revival break out. We have seen very little of it these last few years. Satan has deceived us to think church is about us. It's all about what we should get, not what we need to give up to see the Lord work. After the Lord had taken my jobs away, He spoke to me, "You are mine and so is your time. I want you to tithe your time to Me." Before He spoke this to me, He had me fast and pray for a spiritual cleansing for twenty-eight days, eating nothing with any sugar in it or that tasted sweet. I love sweets. A few weeks later I saw the Lord bring a family member to start growing closer to the Lord. I never dreamed the Lord would use me to do this. Another person came to be mentored in a closer walk with the Lord, and then another came to be mentored.

Back in 1996, I have it journaled, the ladies in the first church I was in told me I needed to write a book. Like Sara in the Bible at her old age was told she was finally going to have a baby. I thought, "Me write a book?" Over the years several people had told me this. I did not realize it then, but I could not write the book when I was first told I would write a book. I still had to live through the many experiences that I have written about here. This book is not about me, it's about my Lord, If He can use a nobody like me, He can use anyone. I am seventy-five years old, and He is still giving me breath. I am looking for what the Lord is going to do next. My heart's desire is to have people see Jesus as real in their lives. He promises to give us our heart's desire, when we love Him with all our hearts. I am claiming that promise.

If you do not know Jesus as your Savior, acknowledge that you need Him, then repent of your sins and ask Him to fill your heart, and take control of your life. If you are at the bottom like I was, He will take you by the hand and lift you up. *(1 Corinthians 2:9, But as it is written, what no eye has seen, no ear has heard, and no human heart has conceived – God has prepared these things for those who love Him. CSB).* I am here to tell you; it is worth it. There is a song, "I would not take anything for my journey now." I can sing this; I get to walk and talk with my Lord and He talks to me.

> *(Psalms 40:5, Lord my God, You have done many things-Your wondrous works and Your plans for us: none can compare with You. If I were to report and speak of them, they are more than can be told. CSB).*

ACKNOWLEDGEMENTS

J want to thank my husband Mr. James, as I like to call him, for all he had to do while I spent hours writing this book night and day. Not only taking care of me but also our motley crew of animals. My son, Rodney Smith, with whom I am so blessed, because he loves his mom and puts up with me and all my computer issues. He has had to teach me how to turn on a computer and bail me out of all the messes I seem to get into. The Lord, in His sovereignty, knew I was going to need a computer technician in the family. My friend Sandy Evans who came once a week so that we can read and talk about Jesus. The Lord spoke to me through her. I was not being told I was going to write a book someday, as I have been for so many years, I was told I needed to get started now. My daughter Melissa who put in a lot of hours rereading and helping her mom through this book. A friend Heather Schremshock who helped me get off to a start with the book. All who helped me one way or another to make this book possible. I thank all my family and friends that encouraged me and prayed me through the writing of this book.

Most of all I thank my Lord. I had been told by so many people over the years that I should write a book but did not think it would ever happen. He inspired me and spoke to me to write this book. He kept pouring into my mind what to write. He led me into each of these situations and circumstances to actually teach me that He truly is a Sovereign God. This book is not about me, it is all about my Lord and what He can do.

Oswald Chambers Devotional Oct 14…

The key to the missionary's work is the authority of Jesus Christ, not the needs of the lost. We are inclined to look on our Lord as one who assists us in our endeavors for God. Yet our Lord places Himself as the absolute sovereign and supreme Lord over His disciples. He does not say that the lost will never be saved if we do not go – He simply says, "Go therefore and make disciples of all the nations…" He says, "Go on the basis of the revealed taught of My sovereignty, teaching and preaching out of your living experience of Me."

CPSIA information can be obtained
at www.ICGtesting.com
Printed in the USA
FSHW021204121121
86166FS